LIVE
Confidently

Confidently

HOW TO KNOW
GOD'S WILL

Michael R. Tucker

TYNDALE
House Publishers, Inc.
Wheaton, Illinois

COVERDALE
House Publishers, Ltd.
Eastbourne, England

LIBRARY OF CONGRESS CATALOG CARD NUMBER 75-37235
ISBN 8423-2216-7, PAPER
COPYRIGHT © 1976 BY TYNDALE HOUSE PUBLISHERS, INC.
WHEATON, ILLINOIS 60187. ALL RIGHTS RESERVED.
FIRST PRINTING, JANUARY 1976
PRINTED IN THE UNITED STATES OF AMERICA

Dedicated to
Mark, Haddon and Shannon
my precious three
who continually teach me
a great deal about
God's will

Preface

This is without doubt the question most frequently asked of any Christian leader. Old Christians, young Christians, new Christians, experienced Christians, adult Christians, teenage Christians, all want the answer to that important question. Long ago those who sponsor Christian conferences found out that when they title a workshop "How To Know God's Will," they better provide the largest room in the building.

It is my intention in this volume to get to the nitty-gritty of the Christian life. An honest attempt has been made to be as blunt as the Bible, without being offensive. The information here is as relevant as today's news. The book grew out of constant questions about the topics which are the chapter titles. It is my opinion that the biblical answers discussed here are necessary for your happiness.

The book is designed for one who needs an overview of the will of God. The recommended reading lists at the end of the chapters are not necessarily books used as references for the work. These lists are suggested to help you dig further into the topic at hand. Discussion questions at the end of each chapter may prove useful to groups.

I don't expect you to agree with all that is written between these covers. But be fair and ask the right question. The issue is not whether you agree with me. Don't whine, "I was never taught that way" or, "My denomination doesn't believe that." The only issue for the true Christian is, "Does the Bible teach that?" Evaluate this material in light of that question.

All honest men admit that they think, act, and write from a set of presuppositions as a base of operation. I openly admit that my observations are based upon the conviction that Jesus Christ is the unique Son of God. Walking on our planet in human form, he gave up his life as a ransom for the sins of all men of all time.

Another presupposition of this material is that the Bible is the infallible Word of God. Its original autographs were without error. The science of textual criticism has given to us accurate translations of those manuscripts so that we still have the Word of God in its essential form. The Bible was written to be believed and lived.

It is my prayer that this book will help you discover God's will more fully for your life, and that you may know Christ and serve him in a greater way.

God's Will and How to Know It

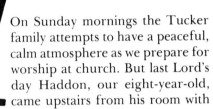

On Sunday mornings the Tucker family attempts to have a peaceful, calm atmosphere as we prepare for worship at church. But last Lord's day Haddon, our eight-year-old, came upstairs from his room with rock music blaring on his portable radio. "Turn that off," I grumped. "Wow!" he sighed, "a guy can't even listen to the radio around here." Did I handle that situation wisely?

Frank is married and has two children. His dad is trying to register his camper in another state so he won't have to pay so much in taxes. Frank believes that's dishonest and said so. His dad rejected Frank's suggestion. What should Frank do?

Chris wanted to know if Christian parents should assume that their children are Christians, and if parents should relate to their children with Christian principles of child-raising even if the children are not yet Christians.

Leslie told me that she had been rejected for the postgraduate art courses for which she had applied. She graduates from college in a few weeks and doesn't even have a lead on a job. What should she do?

Jim was wondering what to do about his wife's ex-husband, who had been giving the family a hard time.

Tom talked with me about the possibility of going to a mission field to use his skill as a mason. His present job is about over and he doesn't know where to go next.

Our five-year-old woke up from her afternoon nap and said she didn't want to go to choir. She usually enjoys choir, yet we dislike forcing the children to participate in church activities. Should we let her miss just this once? Insist that she attend?

As a parent and pastor I'm constantly looking for God's will in my life, the life of my family, and the lives of many others. How do I discover God's will? That's the crucial question.

Six principles stand out in any Christian's search for God's will in his/her life:

1. Evaluate the prerequisites.
2. Don't expect lightning bolts.
3. Collect and evaluate all available information.
4. See God's control.
5. Be sensitive to God's timing.
6. Look for the signposts.

Let's examine these pointers individually.

Evaluate the prerequisites. Determining God's will for your life requires a plan of attack. The first and foremost factor in this plan is a study of God's Word. There are many specifics in the Word of God which help us determine his will for our lives. For instance, the Bible clearly teaches that it is never right to lie, cheat, or commit adultery. The many black and white rules of the Bible are very helpful. Of course, we only know those rules as we read and understand them in their context. But the Bible does not give specific answers to all of our contemporary issues. But where we do not have a black and white rule, we always have several principles directly from the Bible that will help us in determining what course of action we should or should not take.

There are three prerequisites to determining God's will. First, be in good physical condition. Don't try to determine God's will regarding a major decision if you are just recuperating from the flu. People who are run down physically easily make mistakes in determining God's will spiritually.

Second, be in good emotional health. Christians sometimes make bad judgments spiritually because they are emotionally immature. Christians should be those who take a realistic approach to life and should be able to cope with life emotionally.

Third, be in good shape spiritually. Unless you are maintaining a proper fellowship with God on a daily basis, you cannot expect to understand his will for your life. Do not be guilty of just running to God when you are in trouble. Maintain a close walk with him throughout every day, and you will discover that it will help you to understand his leading in your life.

Don't expect lightning bolts. "Dramatic" answers to prayers are often shared among the members of the body of Christ in our church. But we must realize that God leads differently in different believers' lives. This can be seen from even a casual reading of the Scriptures.

It is always encouraging to hear a new believer share God's answers to prayer in his life. "Lightning bolts" often seem to strike all around him. The reason for this seems to be that a baby Christian or a Christian inexperienced in searching for God's will needs dramatic leading in order to get God's message. He has problems knowing if what he "feels" is God speaking, Satan speaking, or his own selfish desires making themselves known. In other words, he can't trust that still, small voice. He usually doesn't know Scripture well enough to dig into its pages to find specific answers quickly enough to help him. So God seems to most often lead through unmistakable circumstances.

It sometimes seems easier for the new convert to discover God's will. When he thinks that God may want him to serve on a mission field, he gets fired from his job one day, and two days later the mission board writes him and requests his services. He asks God to give him someone to witness to, and his roommate knocks at the door and asks if he will tell him about the Lord.

Chuck needed some money to tide him over until his G.I. Bill check came to help him with his expenses as a student. He applied for a loan from the government credit union since he had recently retired from the military. He was told to return the next day to pick up the money. That afternoon Chuck prayed that if he shouldn't obligate himself with the loan, God would somehow stop him. In a few hours a phone call came from a state official in Nevada, telling Chuck that he had just mailed him a sizable check which he had been trying to claim from the state of Nevada for two years. The exciting part was that the official called at just the right time. Usually such checks would be mailed, and no call would be made.

When Marvin decided to go into the ministry, he asked God to sell his grocery store. In a short time a man walked into the store, made an offer, and in a week owned the store. As the final papers were signed, he commented to Marvin, "I don't know why I did this. I've never even thought of owning a grocery store before."

God often leads in such dramatic ways. But the more mature believer does not expect such dramatic events in his life as the normal means of understanding God's will. Usually God does not lead him through strange and unusual events. Most frequently God leads the mature believer through a quiet, still, small voice. The more mature believer can be trusted to determine God's will through his own heart and mind. The new Christian's heart and mind and conscience cannot be trusted yet, so God leads him in more dynamic ways.

Because the experienced Christian has a history of walking with God and obeying his Word, he is more sensitive to God's voice. He doesn't have so much difficulty sorting out God's voice and Satan's temptations. His own will is accustomed to bending toward God's will, and his desires really do match God's desires. Experience and practice just make it easier for him to discern God's will without the "lightning bolts." He can trust himself to know God's will. He knows Scripture, and he doesn't worry about confusing the context and so getting a wrong message.

Usually when mature Christians need to make major decisions in life, they pray, read the Bible, and do all they can to discover God's will. But sometimes they don't seem to get a clear-cut answer. The alternatives before them seem equal in weight. So they do what they believe is best in that situation. There aren't any emotions that seem to push them either way. Circumstances seem to be similar in all choices. So, they simply ask God not to let them make a mistake, and they plunge into the decision that seems right. And that decision is God's will. That's what God wanted. They made the right decision.

Admittedly this method appears to be more difficult, but it really isn't. The mature Christian must realize that God won't let him make an error in knowing his will. Some Christians act as though God is trying to keep his will hidden from them, as though God is playing a game of seeing if he can keep the shroud over his will while the Christian tries to pull it off and see what the answer is. But God doesn't act like that. He wants his children to know his will. He gladly shows the true seeker what he wants to know.

When Pete and Jan came into the office to discuss their marital problems, I already knew what she was thinking. She was thinking the same thing every Christian thinks when he/she becomes dissatisfied with his/her marriage: I must have been out of God's will when I got married.

My first assignment was to give this couple new hope. They needed hope that they could remain married to each other and be genuinely happy. Unfortunately, most marital problems only stop in at the pastor's office on the way to the attorney to file for divorce (believe it or not, I have had that happen). Jan couldn't point to any "signs" or "wonders" which had definitely showed her eighteen months before that Pete was the one for her. I reminded her that during those days she did have a quiet assurance of God's will. God was leading her as a mature Christian through her heart and mind. She wasn't living in sin. She was honestly seeking God's will. She prayed for God to stop the plans for marriage if she wasn't in his will. So how could she now believe that God had failed her eighteen months earlier? The idea suddenly appeared absurd to her. Certainly her God wasn't like that. Then we were able to get to the root of their marital problems.

Understanding how God leads in different lives is a tremendous advantage for the Christian. It prevents him from expecting God to lead in his life as God leads in someone else's life. It keeps Christians from comparing themselves with one another, a dangerous practice. It prohibits Christians from condemning others too. It allows the body of Christ to accept all members and to accept how they seem to discover God's will.

I have noticed that in our body-life sharing in our church, on the occasions when college students and younger Christians share their current experiences, the older Christians tend to refrain from sharing. Older Christians' testimonies often seem to lack a certain sparkle when compared with God's leading in the younger lives. But when the older, more mature Christians share, the younger Christians refrain because they realize that their experiences seem somewhat shallow when compared to those of the mature Christians.

Please don't get the idea that God never leads in dramatic ways for the mature Christian. That isn't so. Paul not only received a vision at the beginning of his life with Christ, but he also received visions later, telling him to go to Macedonia and assuring him of God's presence and protection.

The Christian life without any drama would be dull. But expecting too many and continued miracles makes for an unstable Christian life. The mature Christian does experience "miracles" and dramatic answers in his life, but these are not the normal way God leads him. A former colleague of mine used to speak of "common, everyday miracles." All of our lives include many such workings of God, but many times we don't even recognize them.

For some months my wife has been suggesting that I need a new suit. Since Nancy selects and purchases all my clothing from the skin out and top to bottom (I heartily approve of that system for our family), she feels the urgency to keep me decently attired. Finally she ordered a suit for me, well aware of the fact that we couldn't afford to pay for it. But Nancy felt that she should do it because God wanted her to do it. She continued to pray for the means to pay for the suit. Last Sunday a man (not a member of our church) handed me a check after the morning service and said, "Pastor, God has instructed me to give you this money to buy a new suit." Nancy doesn't even know the fellow; she had told no one of the need. Praise God! It's exciting to see God zap a few lightning bolts now and then, even for us older Christians.

But there are two sides to every coin. One day I spent a traumatic session with the local city council trying to get approval for a new church building in a certain area of the city. Neighbors opposed us, and the complicated result was that the decision of the city council was unacceptable to us. We were going to release our option on the land and forfeit months of work and planning and money on the project. The property was located in a nice area of town known as Rockrimmon. That very morning I had read that the Benjaminites defeated the Gibeahites who fled to the Rock of Rimmon (Judges 20). Three times in that one chapter the term "Rock of Rimmon" appears. Lightning bolt? Answer to God's will? Leading? God speaking directly to me through his Word? Nope.

None of that. Just a consequence. That was the place I had programmed to read that day, as part of my systematic plan of reading through the Bible every year. Nothing spectacular, just God quietly speaking through the normal principles of Judges 20. I laughed, looked closely, but went on reading, looking for the next principle from the Word that day.

Collect data. In the Sermon on the Mount Jesus tells us how to discover the Father's will: "Ask, and you will be given what you ask for. Seek, and you will find. Knock, and the door will be opened" (Matthew 7:7).

The process is clear. We should first ask that we might be clearly shown what to do. We should pray that we will not misinterpret the signal that is sent. Then we should seek, i.e., gather data.

Many Christians fail here. They expect God to zap them with lightning every time. But God usually uses information to direct us in his will.

Ben was sure that "Miss Perfect" was a certain young lady who had been in our city for the past summer. She had the qualities of character that Ben admired. She was a spiritual person. She was well-balanced in most areas of life, and she was attractive. Ben knew this was it. "Well, Ben," I questioned, "tell me about her. How well do you know her? How much time have you spent with her?" "Frankly," my friend admitted, "I don't really know her very well." In fact, I discovered, he had had only one fifteen-minute private conversation with this girl! They had been in close living, working, and ministering situations on several occasions through the years, but he had not ever had any more personal, private contact than that one brief talk.

My response to that approach is, "Nonsense." Ben couldn't possibly know if that is the right girl for him to marry. He didn't have enough information. God leads through data. Get the facts. Date her. Get to know her. Then you can discover God's will about the matter.

(By the way, "Miss Perfect" wasn't the one for Ben. In fact, he is marrying another fine Christian girl this month, a girl he has dated, gotten to know and love, and recognizes as God's will for him.)

When you consider any purchase or move, gather facts. Certainly fact-gathering should be done after prayer and as the Christian walks in the Spirit. But it must be done! Don't expect God to lead you without facts. Granted, he does on occasion break his pattern, but not often. The normal, usual way God leads us to understand his will is through the information we have collected.

Then, we are to knock. We should enter in, go forward.

Every Christian must understand that discovering God's will does not bring less effort in the Christian life. Jacques Ellul says:

> We are thus put in a cruel dilemma. God makes His will known to us. We must will it and do it ourselves. We must decide on our own to do it. This is unquestionable. Nevertheless, we must not take over God's Word. We must not substitute our own intention, time, or means for those of God which alone are right and good.[1]

Proverbs 21:31 says, "Go ahead and prepare for the conflict, but victory comes from God." In other words, we must understand God's will as the children of Israel did. Frequently God spoke to their leader and assured him that the day's battle would be won by God. But God also said, "Grab your sword and get going." The Christian is to determine God's will and relax in that; yet that does not mean an escape from activity or even hard work.

See God's control. Discovering God's will shows that he is in

---

[1]Jacques Ellul, *The Politics of God and the Politics of Man* (Grand Rapids, Mich.: Eerdmans, 1972), p. 114.

control. Joseph's brothers sold him into slavery, but Joseph replied to his brothers years later, when they discovered he was the Prime Minister of Egypt, "But don't be angry with yourselves that you did this to me, for God did it. He sent me here ahead of you to preserve your lives" (Genesis 45:5). Joseph told his brothers that it was God's will that had been ultimately worked for the good of all of them.

Surely every growing Christian has seen this kind of activity in his own life. I remember trying for several months to sell our home a few years ago, with no success. However, a few months later, when God wanted us to leave the community and begin a different ministry, our home sold in one day without any difficulty whatsoever. Only when the home sold was I able to see God's will in not allowing us to sell the home a few months before.

And of course, there are events in every Christian's life that he may not be able to fully understand. All Christians face certain difficulties or sicknesses which do not seem to be compatible with the direction in which God wishes them to travel. Yet, that Christian is assured of God's control. It is refreshing to remember that God does not ask us to understand, he only asks us to be faithful. We are comforted when we realize that God's ways are not our ways and that one day we shall understand his will in a more complete manner.

Mordecai told Esther to risk her life and go plead her people's case before the king. "If you keep quiet at a time like this, God will deliver the Jews from some other source, but you and your relatives will die; what's more, who can say but that God has brought you into the palace for just such a time as this?" (Esther 4:14). Frequently we are able to determine God's will and so to see God's control. It is good to remember as we go through a problem or crisis that there is a good chance that we will one day be able to look back at that situation, thank God, and say, "So that's what God was trying to teach me back there!"

Be sensitive to God's timing. God usually reveals a little of his will for our lives at a time. Understanding God's will may be like seeing headlights of a car shine into the night. As one travels forward, the headlights reveal more of the road before him. As passengers in the car, we can't see very far ahead of us. But God sees the entire road and journey from a different perspective.

When Mt. Rushmore was being completed, the workers often complained about noticeable imperfections in the images of Presidents Washington, Lincoln, Jefferson, and Roosevelt. That was certainly true from where the workmen were stationed. But standing back at a distance, one could see the whole scene in its exactness and beauty. In our problems we are sometimes so close to the situation that we can't see God's glory through the circumstances. But it is helpful to be able to step back and see God's master plan from his point of view.

God's will must also be done in God's time. When Israel refused to go into the land of Canaan (Numbers 13, 14), God promised to punish them. When they heard that announcement, they repented and said they would go to battle immediately. God responded by telling them to wait. But they charged into the battle anyway and were soundly defeated. God's will must be compatible with God's timing.

Look for the signposts. God does not intend for the discovery of his will to involve groping in the darkness. Signposts can point us to the will of God. But remember, these are only valid if several point in the same direction.

Inner urgings. Most often God leads his mature followers through an inner urging by the Holy Spirit. Some call this God's leading through the heart; others refer to one's mind; another may refer to the conscience. The point is that God simply leads in a quiet, inner way.

Desires. Many times Christians can find God's will by simply asking, "What do I want to do?" But some of our desires are selfish. Even a mature believer must be very cautious about this signpost.

Advice. It is always wise in seeking God's will to ask the advice of a mature Christian whom you respect. Be cautious about asking advice of those who are not Christians, and be cautious about asking too many people for advice. It is true that there is wisdom in a multitude of counselors, but one can overdo it.

Common sense. Many times God just leads through the believer's common sense, though he sometimes leads us contrary to what our reasoning tells us.

Circumstanèes. Be very careful about this one. Christians are more often out of balance on this signpost than any other. Many Christians talk about open and closed doors. What they mean is that circumstances seem to show them what they ought to do. Remember, God is not the only superhuman person in the universe who can open and close doors and try to direct your life through circumstances. When I publicly declared my intentions to follow God's will into vocational Christian service, my best friend did the same. A short while later, circumstances allowed this young man to purchase a car which he had wanted for some time. It seemed at the time that God was opening the door for the purchase. That automobile, however, prevented him on a number of occasions from ever entering school to receive training for vocational ministry. It now appears that someone else must have opened that door.

At one point in King Saul's life, he thought he had David trapped and he said, "God has delivered David into my hand." He had just finished killing eighty-five of God's priests, and now he was trying to murder David. Obviously the circumstances were not being arranged by God.

Glorifying God. Always ask yourself, "What will glorify God the most?" What would glorify God most as far as short-range goals are concerned? What would glorify God the most in my life right now if I took a certain course of action in determining God's will? But also look at the long-range goals God may have for your life. It may glorify God most in a short-range goal for you to go to a foreign country to be a missionary, but perhaps training and education would glorify God the most long-range.

Unity. A man from another state called me long-distance to talk about his daughter, who was living in our area at the time. During our conversation, his wife got onto another phone and began loudly insulting me, apparently for no reason. I told the gentleman that I would continue to talk with him, but his wife must leave the conversation. At that point he angrily accused me of talking with another man in our church, who (he felt) had filled my mind with evil rumors about his wife. The interesting part of the story is that I had never talked with the other man in our church about this man's wife. I told the gentleman on the telephone that the reason he was getting the same advice from two Christians was that the two Christians had read the same Book. I furthermore suggested to him that when he began to see several Christians giving him the same suggestions, without collaborating with one another, he might consider that perhaps God's will was being revealed to him.

Unity among God's people is frequently an evidence of God's will. But of course, this sign, like all the others, must be taken in conjunction with one or two other signs pointing in the same direction.

Peace. Once you have made a decision about God's will, you should be able to say, "The decision is made. I feel I have made the right decision. I have obeyed biblical principles. I have seen the signposts, and several have pointed to this conclusion and this is what I am going to do." When you feel like the decision is over, whether or not you have actually instituted it, then you should have peace, a relaxed feeling about the issue.

However, if you feel as though you are not quite sure about the decision, and perhaps wonder if you have made the wrong decision, then maybe you need to review your principles of determining God's will. This sign, as with all the others, is frequently misused by Christians who rationalize God's will. I have talked with Christians on a number of occasions who are going in a direction obviously opposed to the will of God revealed through the Bible. Yet these Christians are willing to say, "I have peace about it." A relaxed feeling, a comfortable feeling, an absence of fear is not necessarily an indication of God's will, but it may be if one has sifted that decision through the Word, the prerequisites, and the signposts.

Why should the Christian be concerned about the will of God anyway? There are at least six reasons:

1. We love him.
2. Life runs more smoothly when we do his will.
3. There are rewards for doing his will.
4. There is punishment for not doing his will.
5. We should be good examples.
6. We don't want to be ashamed when we meet Christ at his return.

Every true believer has a deep, warm love for Jesus Christ. That's part of the believer's new nature. Jesus said, "If you love me, obey me" (John 14:15). He also taught, "I will only reveal myself to those who love me and obey me. The Father will love them too, and we will come to them and live with them. Anyone who doesn't obey me doesn't love me. And remember, I am not making up this answer to your question! It is the answer given by the Father who sent me" (John 14:23, 24).

The only reason we are able to love is because God first loved us. The original text of 1 John 4:19 doesn't say that "we love *him* because he first loved us." It literally reads that "we love, because he first loved us." The only reason we are able to love God, or anyone, is because God acted first. He loved us even when we were far from him in rebellion against his purposes for our lives.

So the true Christian wants to know God's will for his life because he loves God. The true Christian understands love and wants to respond in love toward God. His motivation is not fear of punishment if he doesn't. His motivation is appreciation for what God has already done for him.

Many reported that they wept as they read about Jenny's death in Erich Segal's best-selling novel *Love Story.* Yet the love between Jenny and her husband, Oliver, was a selfish love. They loved only each other. They were crass materialists. They were immoral. They did not have love and concern for others, good, or God.

The Christian is different. Simply because he is a new creation in Christ (2 Corinthians 5:17) he loves God. He desires to serve others. He commits his life to performing good works. And he is busily trying to discover and put into practice God's will. Rollo May declared that "hate is not the opposite of love, apathy is." [2] Christians who are not searching for God's will show they don't love God. Jesus said that the Christian who loves him obeys him, and that means we should understand what he wants us to do.

Another reason we want to understand God's will is that life runs more smoothly when one walks with God. That is not to say that one has fewer problems. That is not to say that spiritual Christians don't suffer the same illnesses, accidents, tragedies as non-Christians. But it is to say that God does watch over his children and give them happy, meaningful lives. The Christian's life is not happy because he is without difficulties, but in spite of his difficulties. Peter put it this way, "The Lord is watching his children, listening to their prayers" (1 Peter 3:12).

Personally, I believe that the Christian who walks closely with God does have fewer frustrations in life. Because he wisely uses his time, God removes the frustrating little matters of life that gobble up so much time. The people he wants to see happen to be in when he calls. He isn't unnecessarily interrupted quite so often. He

---

[2]Rollo May, *Love and Will* (New York: W. W. Norton and Co., 1969), p. 29.

finds what he is looking for in the stockroom or store without wasted time. God just honors his life.

Jerry is an accomplished teacher at the U. S. Air Force Academy. He has a Ph.D., specializing in lasers. He is also heavily involved as a Sunday school superintendent in a local church. One semester he was really frustrated because new responsibilities, additional assignments, and various pressures at work caused him to get behind in some of his responsibilities at church. He didn't want to do less at church, but he saw no alternative. Then he decided to rethink his priorities. Jerry decided that God's work was more important than man's work. Although he continued to do an excellent job at his office and in the classroom, the Sunday school work was placed high on the priority list. And, amazingly, he has time for both, plus more time for his family.

Because the Christian who walks on the path of God's will is given wisdom and granted answers to his prayers, he doesn't make so many mistakes in his life, work, and ministry. He simply doesn't offend others quite so often. Thus he has less to straighten out later. And, of course, others cooperate with him more readily. So you would expect smoother living in each area of his experience.

A further reason the true Christian wants to know God's will is that there are rewards for understanding and doing it. Although we don't earn our salvation (Ephesians 2:8, 9), we will be recompensed for doing good after salvation. "If the work which any man built on the foundation survives, he will receive a reward" (1 Corinthians 3:14, RSV).

In fact, the Bible lists at least four different crowns or rewards which will be given to Christians for faithfully following God's will. They are: the incorruptible crown (1 Corinthians 9:25), for those who exercise self-denial and self-control; the crown of righteousness (2 Timothy 4:8), for those who love the prospect of Christ's return; the crown of life, for those who endure testings (James 1:12) and for those who die as martyrs for Christ (Revelation

2:10); and the crown of glory (1 Peter 5:2-4), for those who diligently shepherd God's flock.

Some seem to reject the idea of working for rewards. Yet the Bible clearly says that God will work on that basis. Of course, the true Christian does not work *only* or *primarily* for rewards. His primary motive is his love for God. But at the same time it is a basic drive and characteristic of man to be motivated by the promise of payment for his struggle.

A lesser motivating factor, yet still important, is that Christians desire to do God's will because there is punishment if we don't. That may appear to be an inferior motive, but the Bible does warn us of the possibility.

"And have you quite forgotten the encouraging words God spoke to you, his child? He said, 'My son, don't be angry when the Lord punishes you. Don't be discouraged when he has to show you where you are wrong. For when he punishes you, it proves that he loves you. When he whips you it proves you are really his child' " (Hebrews 12:5, 6).

Discipline from God is a serious matter. We must avoid it at all costs. It's true that God forgives sin, any sin, when it is confessed. But forgiveness doesn't erase history. The alcoholic who is converted and quits drinking still has liver and heart trouble. The Christian who sins may put scars on his soul which will last the rest of his life. Some Christians are still suffering the natural consequences of sins commited years ago. God has forgiven those sins, and he is not directly punishing them, but a person reaps what he sows (Galatians 6:7).

Every true Christian wants to be a good example. He cannot do that unless he makes a habit of doing God's will for his life. Paul complimented the Christians in Thessalonica because they had discovered God's will and were model Christians. "Then you yourselves became an example to all the other Christians in Greece" (1 Thessalonians 1:7).

Reader's Digest [3] has reported that fat dog-owners are likely to have fat dogs. A study conducted at an animal hospital in Grimsby, England, indicates, not surprisingly, that if the owner does not exercise or eat properly, neither will his dog. More than one-fourth of the dogs examined were obese. More important, our example affects our children, our husbands and wives, and all those who are closest to us.

Joan, a teen-ager, came to see me the month I started my present ministry as a pastor in Colorado Springs. [4] She was confused. The church had recently gone through ugly in-fighting in dismissing its pastor, attempting to call another man, splitting again, generally performing very badly. Joan told me about sitting in a business meeting and hearing Christians express their bitterness toward each other (and haranguing movie attendance, a traditional but unfounded taboo in many Christian circles). These negative examples hindered Joan's faith. An ounce of practice is worth a pound of preach.

Others in the church do watch your life. Your family (and even your dog?) do examine your behavior. So be a good example, know God's will for your life. Without that knowledge you will stumble through life and trip others also.

Mr. David Gill tells how he once disappointed his Christian parents when he took part in a school play where his four lines included using the Lord's name in a vain manner. [5] He felt very much ashamed. My first meeting with Bob, a young man in his mid-twenties, came the weekend after he had been arrested for a felony. We met together weekly for several months as he began to grow in the Christian life. But Bob would never talk about the legal charges against him. Finally, it was necessary for me

---

[3]"Notes from All Over," *Reader's Digest,* October 1973, p. 80. Originally appeared in *Family Health Magazine.*
[4]See author's book *The Church That Dared to Change* (Wheaton, Ill.: Tyndale House Publishers, Inc., 1975).
[5]Virginia Hearn (editor), *What They Did Right* (Wheaton, Ill.: Tyndale House Publishers, Inc., 1974), p. 15.

to talk to the District Attorney to help Bob by being a character reference for him. The D.A. explained the charges—child molesting. It seemed clear that Bob was guilty.

The biggest problem in the case was that Bob would not admit his guilt or even talk about the situation. I had to confront him with it. Through a long, grueling, tear-soaked session, Bob admitted to me his guilt. His hang-up was obvious—shame. His guilt was gone, he had confessed that to God. He was forgiven, he was sure about that. But the awful shame of the act hung over him like a ominous, black cloud.

Feeling ashamed is an emotion we all want to avoid. And that's another good reason to know God's will. "And now, my little children, stay in happy fellowship with the Lord so that when he comes you will be sure that all is well, and will not have to be ashamed and shrink back from meeting him" (1 John 2:28).

After another soul-grabbing session with a man who confessed his sin, he sighed, "I'm so tired." Sam explained that he wasn't physically tired. He wasn't tired of trying to live life, or even the Christian life. He sobbed, "I'm just tired of disappointing him." That's good motivation to walk with God.

As Christians, we want to know the will of God. And as Christians, we *can* know and live the will of God. Our heavenly Father is not hiding his blueprint for our lives. He loves us, and he knows that without making a habit of doing his will, we can't be happy or complete.

Every Christian who wants the will of God ought to be willing to pray, "Dear God, I want your will, nothing more, nothing less, nothing else."

DISCUSSION QUESTIONS

1. What are some dramatic ways God has led in your life?

2. How do you determine the balance between praying for God's direction and being busy discovering God's will?

3. What are some unanswered prayers you have prayed in the past that you now recognize to be God's leading?

4. By which signposts does God seem to direct you most often?

5. How do you know that your decision is God's will?

SUGGESTED READING

How to Choose Your Life's Work, Clyde M. Narramore. Zondervan, 1969.

Discovering the Will of God, G. Christian Weiss. Back to the Bible Broadcast, 1971.

God's Will Made Clear, Mrs. Paul Friederichsen. Moody Press, 1960.

God's Will Is Not Lost, John MacArthur Jr. Victor Books, 1973.

Where Do I Go from Here, God?, Zac Poonen. Tyndale House, 1972.

God's Will and Counting the Cost

Leroy is a Christian businessman who owns and operates a fence company. He knows that there are ways to cut his costs by using inferior materials. Probably none of his customers would know the difference, and he would make more profit. But he refuses, preferring to be a Christian businessman rather than a businessman who happens to be a Christian.

Earl's neighbor wants to give him a free sack of fertilizer for his lawn. But Earl knows that the fertilizer was illegally taken from his neighbor's employer. All the employees seem to be involved. The boss knows it, he just turns his back while people load up whatever they need. They figure that the employer, the United States government, doesn't miss it anyway. Earl says, "No, thanks."

Leroy and Earl are Christians who really want God's will in their lives. And they realize that doing God's will involves some very practical costs.

Jesus never looks for part-time disciples. He isn't interested in those who only half-heartedly commit themselves to his cause. So the Christian who says he wants to know God's will better be prepared for a life-challenging revelation. The Lord spoke clearly on the subject. He didn't stutter or timidly address the crowds.

> Great crowds were following him. He turned around and addressed them as follows: "Anyone who wants to be my follower must love me far more than he does his own father, mother, wife, children, brothers, or sisters—yes, more than his own life—otherwise he cannot be my disciple. And no one can be my disciple who does not carry his own cross and follow me. But don't begin until you count the cost. For who would begin construction of a building without first getting estimates and then checking to see if he has enough money to pay the bills? Otherwise he might complete only the foundation before running out of funds. And then how everyone would laugh!" (Luke 14:25-29)

Those are the words of the New Testament, but a man of the Old Testament provides us with an outstanding example of one who counted the cost, made the right decision, and enjoyed God's best.

About 400 years after the Flood, 300 years after the tower of Babel, there was a wealthy businessman living in Ur, near the Persian Gulf. He was involved in the import-export business. His name was Terah, and he had three sons, Abraham, Haran, and Nahor (Genesis 11).

"Genesis" means beginning. We have in this book the beginning of the human race in Adam, the beginning of the human race again in Noah, and now the beginning of the chosen race through Abraham.

Abraham is one of the most important men in history. The first eleven chapters of Genesis cover more than 2,000 years. The last thirty-nine chapters of Genesis concern only about 400 years. The first eleven chapters concern the whole human race. But the last thirty-nine chapters concern only one man, his son, his grandson, and his great-grandson (Abraham, Isaac, Jacob, and Joseph).

The rest of the Old Testament concerns the family of this one man. And the New Testament begins by introducing God's Son, Jesus Christ, the son of David, the son of Abraham. Abraham's name occurs in fifteen Old Testament books, and twelve New Testament books. He is claimed as the father of the Jews, Muslims, and Christians. He is the only man in Scripture to be called "the friend of God."

Abraham received God's best because he was willing to follow God's will. One of the reasons you have chosen to read this book is that you, too, are interested in discovering God's will. There are several lessons which we can learn from the friend of God which will help us in our search for God's best.

God's will may involve hardship for your life. Abraham was probably very comfortable in Ur, where God first spoke to him (Acts 7:2). His Hebrew name meant "a wealthy caravaneer." His wife's name, Sarah, means "princess." Perhaps she was in prominent social standing. Abraham had no reason, as far as we know, to wish to leave Ur. There undoubtedly were plenty of heathen in Ur, and Abraham could have reasoned that he could do enough for God there. Why would God want him to go somewhere else? His friends and relatives probably called him foolish and fanatical for wanting to travel to who knows where. After all, "religion can be carried too far."

Abraham was undoubtedly barraged with friendly advice which expounded the dangers of the deserts and the fierceness of other peoples. Sarah's mother perhaps didn't want her to go. Some of the family was finally successful in convincing Abraham to take things a little slower.

Abraham did not completely obey God's will at first. Genesis 11:31, 32 report that Terah took Abraham from

Ur to Haran, which was the jumping off place to go into the desert toward Canaan. And Abraham stayed there, perhaps for as long as fifteen years. Someone had convinced him not to go to extremes, but to only go halfway with God's will.

Every true Christian needs to face the fact that God's will may involve hardships for his life. There may be friends and relatives who will try to get you to compromise on what you know to be God's best for you. Some of the same arguments used will be those which kept Abraham from completely serving God for many years.

There were numerous reasons Abraham could have given to stay where he was. There was only one reason to go: the call of God. And yet, that one reason tipped the scales in favor of what was right for him. Each Christian must learn to identify God's tap on the shoulder. When you respond in faith to that tap, God will show you his will for your life.

God's will always involves promises for the Christian. After Abraham obeyed God and left Haran, God gave additional promises (Genesis 12:1-3). It is a principle of the Bible that when we live up to our present understanding of God's will, he gives us more information. When we do not do what we know to do, often God will withhold further enlightenment. Probably some Christians have not heard from God in years. (God has been speaking, they just haven't been listening.) These Christians may read the Bible and even pray. But they do not have any real experience of definite direction from God. Maybe they are not even convicted about this. God has spoken but they have not obeyed. God is waiting for obedience before he will speak further.

There are many Bible promises which go with every tap on the shoulder. Jesus said, "I will never leave you nor forsake you." God has promised, "I will meet all your needs according to my riches in glory by Christ Jesus." The Bible comforts us with the words, "Greater is he that is within you than he that is in the world."

In the faith chapter of the Bible, Hebrews 11, more space is given to Abraham than to anyone else. God's will for him did involve hardships. But it also involved God's promises. By faith Abraham obeyed. As Christians are willing to obey God by faith, he will lead them into his will and into his best for their lives.

God's will also involves God's enriching your life. Just look at what Abraham would have missed if he had not obeyed. If Abraham had failed to do God's will, you would have asked as you read this chapter, "Abraham who?" No one would ever have heard of Abraham of Ur had not Abraham stepped forward into the desert by faith. Abraham's children are the best-known kids in the whole world. Abraham's life was rewarded for doing God's will.

He also had fulfillment in his life. Perhaps he would have been richer had he stayed in Mesopotamia. But perhaps not, for we know he was a very wealthy man in Palestine. We also know that following God gave him peace and purpose. He probably would have had a dull life in Mesopotamia. His life in Palestine was an exciting and enriching experience.

Why did God call Abraham? Why not Nahor or Haran? Why did God call Martin Luther? Why not any one of the hundreds of other captive priests? Why did God call Paul? Why not Gamaliel, or Annas, or Caiphas? And why has God tapped you on the shoulder? The answer is grace, pure grace! (Of course, it's also true that God may have called others, but they didn't dare obey.)

God wants to give you a barrel of blessings. Understand that God's will may involve hardships. Count the cost first. Then go by faith into whatever he wants you to do. With God's will there is the promise of protection and guidance. And with his will always goes his blessing. Pay attention to that divine tap on your shoulder.

DISCUSSION QUESTIONS

1. What are some examples in your life of God leading contrary to "common sense?"

2. What do you consider God's calling in your life to be? When did that occur? How are you doing in fulfilling that "tap on the shoulder?"

3. If you are not moving in the direction God has called you, why not? What are some positive steps you could take this week to move closer to God's will for your life?

4. Recount some benefits you have already seen in your life as a result of obeying God's will.

5. What are some "hardships" you have faced as a result of obeying God's will?

SUGGESTED READING

A Call to Christian Character, Bruce Shelley (Editor). Zondervan, 1970.
The Great Conflict, Ethel Barrett. Regal Books, 1969.
Song of Abraham, Ellen Gunderson Traylor. Tyndale House, 1973. (Novel)
The Cost of Discipleship, Dietrich Bonhoeffer. Macmillan, 1967.

God's Will and Continuing to Grow

Mankind can be grouped into the rich and the poor, the haves and the have-nots, the liberals and the conservatives, the elite and the hoi polloi. The Greeks classified humanity as Greeks and barbarians. The Jews use the terms Jews and Gentiles. Some teen-age boys are classified by teen-age girls as those with a car and those without a car. The guys classify the gals as those who are sharp and those who are "ugh." Adults are categorized by youth as those who are with it and those who are not.

Our heavenly Father categorizes us. First Corinthians 2:14 speaks of the natural man, the man who is alienated and apart from God, the man who has no capacity for spiritual things. The natural man cannot understand spiritual truth. No matter how intelligent or educated he (or she) is, he cannot understand the Bible and its spiritual message.

The second category of mankind is listed in verse 15—the spiritual man. This man has a spiritual capacity. He has responded to God's love and grace, and has given his life to Christ. This man has the Holy Spirit to instruct him in spiritual matters.

Not all Christians are spiritual. See 1 Corinthians 3:1-4, Hebrews 5, and 1 Peter 2. Christians can be either spiritual or carnal. And, sadly, carnal Christians don't grow.

In 1 Corinthians 3:1, 2, Paul demonstrates that new Christians are babies: "Dear brothers, I have been talking to you as though you were still just babies in the Christian life, who are not following the Lord, but your own desires; I cannot talk to you as I would to healthy Christians, who are filled with the Spirit. I have had to feed you with milk and not with solid food."

Paul's illustration here fits the analogy of Jesus in John 3. In that chapter Jesus says that everyone who wants to know God must be born again, must receive a new life and new nature from God. One is no longer a natural man; he accepts new values and goals when he turns his life over to Jesus Christ.

All human beings begin as natural men. At some point in every man's life, he makes a decision to accept Christ as Lord and Savior over his life, or to reject Christ. The person who rejects Christ remains a natural man and shall forever be apart from God; he leaves this world in that state. The one who responds to God is termed a spiritual man. But the spiritual man begins his new life as a baby.

A new Christian, a baby Christian, needs to be fed with milk. Our newborn son had a birth defect which necessitated an operation when we could get him to weigh ten pounds. I figured there's nothing that will help a child grow strong and healthy as fast as a hamburger. So I fed him a Big Mac. Ridiculous! Had I tried that, the baby would have rejected the solid food, and my wife would have clubbed me with a skillet. We all know that babies begin with milk. New Christians are to begin on the milk of the Word, Paul told the Corinthians.

Please remember that there are not some milk doctrines and some meat doctrines. The reference to milk as contrasted with meat does not mean that there are some doctrines a new Christian cannot handle. Rather, the reference seems to indicate that there are some depths of some of the Bible's teachings that a new Christian cannot handle. For instance, salvation is not a milk doctrine, while prophecy is a meat doctrine. Salvation has some deep truths which new Christians cannot handle at first. Also, prophecy has some very easy truths that even a baby Christian can grasp. The issue is depth, not breadth.

This analogy may also refer to the communication of truth. A baby has a short attention span. The teacher may need to go more slowly and use more aids to assist the new Christian.

No one blames a baby for being a baby, as long as he doesn't remain a baby. A carnal Christian is a baby Christian who should no longer be a baby, who should have grown beyond infancy.

Babies (and Christians) are supposed to grow. In Paul's words, "For you are still only baby Christians, controlled by your own desires, not God's. When you are jealous of one another and divide up into quarreling groups, doesn't that prove you are still babies, wanting your own way?" (1 Corinthians 3:3).

Continued babyhood brings complacency toward spiritual truth. Notice that Paul did not condemn baby Christians in verse one for not understanding. But he did come down hard on Christians who should be beyond babyhood but aren't. Continued babyhood is carnality and so is displeasing to God.

A carnal Christian is different from a baby Christian. There are two Greek words in the passage which show the difference. The word *sarkinos* may be translated "fleshy," or more specifically, "composed of flesh." The Greek word in verse three is *sarkikos*, which may be translated "fleshly," or "controlled by flesh." Verse 1 speaks of the new Christian who can't understand the Bible too well when he studies it. He is fleshy. Verse 3 refers to the person who has been a Christian for some time and simply does not attempt to study the Bible and its truth.

He is fleshly. There is a great difference between being fleshy and fleshly.

To the world, a carnal Christian is the same as a natural man. He has no effective prayer life. He has no effective witness to his community. He has no systematic plan for studying the Scriptures. He may attend church, and he may be a nice person. But to the world, he appears the same as the man who is totally without Christ.

A carnal Christian is certainly a detriment to God's cause in the world. I once spoke with a man who told me that he would rather go to hell than spend eternity with ninety percent of the people who call themselves Christians. That's what carnal Christians will do for a man.

Some people have the mistaken idea that sitting under the Word makes spiritual Christians. It doesn't. The Christian who listens to tapes, takes notes, and travels to summer conferences to hear great sermons from great preachers may still be a carnal Christian. The Word of God is of value only if we live it.

Spiritual growth can be measured, but not in terms of chronological age. Some saints are still talking about how long they have been a Christian—"God saved me in 1952." Great. What is he doing in your life today? Twenty-three times zero is still zero.

Spiritual growth can be measured by our relationship with others. Paul writes, "For while one saith, I am of Paul; and another, I am of Apollos; are ye not carnal?" (1 Corinthians 3:4, KJV). Exalting oneself while condemning others is a sign of carnality. Bickering and pettiness are signs of carnality. The Christian's walk among men illustrates his walk with God.

In Hebrews 5 we have another measuring stick—the amount of knowledge a Christian has. We read:

"You have been Christians a long time now, and you ought to be teaching others, but instead you have dropped back to the place where you need someone to teach you all over again the very first principles in God's Word. You are like babies who can drink only milk, not old enough for solid food. And when a person is still living on milk it shows he isn't very far along in the Christian life, and doesn't know much about the difference between right and wrong. He is still a baby-Christian!

"You will never be able to eat solid spiritual food and understand the deeper things of God's Word until you become better Christians and learn right from wrong by practicing doing right" (verses 12-14).

Spiritual babies often ask, "Is this activity right? Is it OK for Christians to do this?" Certainly there is no problem with baby Christians asking others to help them in making decisions. But Christians who should be well along the path of spiritual growth shouldn't be asking baby questions.

Every Christian needs to ask himself whether or not he is a carnal Christian. How do you measure up to God's standards? Hebrews 6:1-3 gives us more information on this:

"Let us stop going over the same old ground again and again, always teaching those first lessons about Christ. Let us go on instead to other things and become mature in our understanding, as strong Christians ought to be. Surely we don't need to speak further about the foolishness of trying to be saved by being good, or about the necessity of faith in God; you don't need further instruction about baptism and spiritual gifts and the resurrection of the dead and eternal judgment. The Lord willing, we will go on now to other things."

The writer to the Hebrews is telling us to get into the Word, be involved in good works, and be patient. Growth takes time. In this same passage (verses 4-6), there is a warning for those who don't grow:

"There is no use trying to bring you back to the Lord again if you have once understood the Good News and tasted for yourself the good things of heaven and shared in the Holy Spirit, and know how good the Word of God is, and felt the mighty powers of the world to come, and then have turned against God. You cannot bring yourself to repent again if you have nailed the Son of God to the cross again by rejecting him, holding him up to mocking and to public shame."

The writer is saying here that it is not possible to lose your salvation and then start over. If you are a genuine Christian, what you sow you must reap. There is no way to abandon the mistakes caused by carnal living in the past by entering into a "new" Christian life a second or third time. But you can change from being a carnal Christian to being a spiritual one.

Do you ever get tired of playing church? Then quit that game. From now on, be serious with God. If you are a carnal Christian, you know it and God knows it too. Sooner or later your actions will demonstrate your carnality to the world.

Carnal Christians don't grow. But they can reverse their growth patterns with God's help. That's a big decision. You need to think about it very carefully.

DISCUSSION QUESTIONS

1. What are some of the characteristics of the carnal person?

2. What is the difference between a fleshly Christian and a fleshy Christian?

3. Are you able to handle the "meat" portions of the Bible's teachings? How do you know?

4. As God categorizes people, where do you fit? Are you happy with this? What are some specific steps you could take this week to improve your position before God?

5. What is the balance between factual knowledge of the Bible and living what the Bible teaches?

SUGGESTED READING

He That Is Spiritual, Lewis Sperry Chafer. Zondervan, 1970.
Balancing the Christian Life, Charles C. Ryrie. Moody Press, 1969.
Be Filled Now, Roy Hession. Christian Literature Crusade, 1968.
Sit, Walk, Stand, Watchman Nee. Christian Literature Crusade, 1974.
True Spirituality, Francis Schaeffer. Tyndale House, 1972.

God's Will
and Your Mate

After a big dance where all of the dates were arranged by a computer, one coed remarked, "It's a frightening experience, finding out exactly what you deserve." God's guidance on dating and mating easily surpasses that of any computer. His knowledge and his love are without limit.

In a recent survey, only twenty-four percent of the women and fourteen percent of the men said that their date had to be of the same religion. But fifty-five percent expressed a desire for a good dancer. A lasting marriage, however, takes more than being light on your feet on the ballroom floor. In fact, the perfect marriage is a triangle —each partner loving the other, and both loving Jesus Christ.

Augustine said, "Love God and do as you please." A good marriage occurs when a man and woman each love Christ and one another. In ninety-five percent of the divorce cases, either one or both partners are irreligious or irregular at church. When families attend church regularly and have daily devotions, only one marriage in 500 breaks up. It's trite but true, "Families that pray together, stay together."

If you want your marriage to be made in heaven, it can be, but only on God's terms. The first requirement is that a Christian marry only a Christian. That principle is found throughout the Bible (e.g., Deuteronomy 7:3, 4; 1 Corinthians 7:39; and 2 Corinthians 6:14-16). That last passage says:

"Don't be teamed with those who do not love the Lord, for what do the people of God have in common with the people of sin? How can light live with darkness? And what harmony can there be between Christ and the devil? How can a Christian be a partner with one who doesn't believe? And what union can there be between God's temple and idols? For you are God's temple, the home of the living God, and God has said of you, 'I will live in them and walk among them, and I will be their God and they shall be my people.' "

Obviously this passage isn't speaking only about marriage, but marriage isn't excluded. Notice that Paul makes a statement, then asks five questions. The first two questions involve the nonbeliever; the next one emphasizes God; the last two questions concern the believer. In other words, all three corners of the triangle are damaged when a believer marries a nonbeliever. God's Word is plain. A Christian who wants God's will, will not marry one who is not a Christian.

One reason for this rule is that the unequal yoke is unfair to the unbeliever. It is certainly a wrong way to begin marriage. He won't be able to understand his Christian partner. The Christian possesses two natures. The non-Christian only has one nature, and that one is alienated from God. The unequally yoked marriage can expect fellowship only in the area of the old nature.

The Christian maintaining a proper testimony before his or her marriage will probably (without trying) discourage the unsaved from entering into matrimony. During their dating days, the Christian walking with God will naturally like different things than the non-Christian. The Christian will enjoy studying the Bible. His date who is unsaved will not understand that. The Christian will enjoy worshiping God. The unsaved person won't know the God whom his friend worships and with whom he talks.

Experience shows that the partners in an unequal marriage drift farther and farther apart. The growing Christian draws closer to God; the unsaved partner often becomes more hardened as he continues to reject the gospel. For a child of God to marry a child of the devil, someone has said, is to have Satan for a father-in-law.

Another reason for God's law against an unequal marriage involves what it will do for (or to) the Christian. Israel was warned against the unequal yoke when God said, "Do not intermarry with them, nor let your sons and daughters marry their sons and daughters. That would surely result in your young people's beginning to worship their gods. Then the anger of the Lord would be hot against you and he would surely destroy you" (Deuteronomy 7:3, 4).

Of course, any believer who flirts with the idea of marrying a non-Christian intends to win the unsaved person to Christ. And occasionally that happens. But very seldom. The difficulty for the Christian is to witness when he or she is out of fellowship with God. And the Christian who marries a nonbeliever is (at the time of marriage) out of fellowship with God.

Most often the Christian partner ends up compromising and wandering from God. The problem, of course, is that he has started his marriage on the devil's terms. It may be true that the unsaved partner is a wonderful person. He or she may be kind, gentle, sweet. The person may agree to attend church, but he's different on the inside. His whole system of values will be different; his motivations are different. And the Christian has no guarantee of what that unsaved partner will be like in five years or twenty-five years or whatever.

The most important question you will ever answer is, "Where will I spend eternity?" The next most important question for you may be, "With whom will I spend my most intimate moments in this life?" God certainly favors marriage. He started the whole business (see the early chapters of Genesis). The Bible shows that marriage is not just for parenthood, although that is part of it. Marriage also includes meeting one another's sexual needs, as explained in the next chapter. Marriage should promote mutual love and understanding. The husband and wife who are able to sing one song in Christian harmony make lovely music for the ears of God. Their lives should show forth the love of God to the world.

Dwight Small, in his excellent book *Design for Christian Marriage,* makes a fine distinction between infatuation and love.

Infatuation comes suddenly. Love grows and grows. The week before I was to be married, my boss told me that I knew nothing about love. I was insulted and irritated at his "wisdom." Now, thirteen years later, I am sure that he was right. One can fall into infatuation, but love is the product of growth.

Infatuation comes after a short acquaintance. Only a few characteristics of an individual need be known when one is infatuated. Love, however, is the result of a total evaluation of the other person's character. Love probes deeply.

Infatuation ignores the deep questions about the other person. Love digs deeply.

Infatuation is self-centered. A person expresses this by saying, "I like to be around the other one because he makes me feel good." Love, however, is always other-centered. Remember that true love is more than finding the right person. It is being the right person.

Infatuation sees the other person as a separate entity. Love always emphasizes unity. Love thinks of "we" rather than "I."

Infatuation allows an individual to say that he loves two people at once with the same intensity. Love, however, clearly can love only one person at a time with the intensity that is necessary for a balanced marriage.

Infatuation is insecure. The one who is infatuated must constantly ask the other person, "Do you love me?" One who has truly grown into love is secure in that love with the other person.

Infatuation has an exaggerated image of the other one in the relationship. Infatuation must always think of the girl as a beautiful model with long, flowing hair, or of the man who is muscle-bound and handsome. Love is more realistic. Love may be willing to say, "I know she has protruding teeth," or "I know he is a ninety-five-pound weakling, but I love him just the same." Love does not need to emphasize the physical attractiveness nearly so much as must infatuation.

Any Christian wanting God's will for a future mate should ask some very important questions:

1. Are we socially suited? Do we enjoy the same things? Am I ever embarrassed at the other person's manners?

2. Are we emotionally suited? Are our temperaments compatible? (Be sure to read *Spirit-Controlled Temperament* by Tim LaHaye.)

3. Are we intellectually suited? It is reasonably important that marriage partners be close to one another's intelligence quotient. Please notice that we are not talking here about education, but about intelligence.

4. Are we economically suited? Again the issue is, "Are we reasonably close?" Do we have the same ideas about how to spend money and how to give money? Are our family economic background pictures reasonably in focus with one another?

5. Are our family backgrounds suited? It is important for the couple to discuss who ruled the roost at his/her home.

6. Do our desires for children match one another? How many children do you wish to have? What does your future partner think about discipline of children? Who came from the more strict environment?

7. Do we agree on how to spend our free time? Do we

enjoy the same types of recreation and hobbies?

8. Does each partner feel that he is getting a good deal from the marriage? It is extremely important for each one to feel that he is getting a better deal than he is giving. When one partner feels as though he is really a better catch than the other person he or she is marrying, there is danger ahead. Each person must truly feel that he could not possibly do better than this particular person he is marrying.

9. Do we agree on who Jesus Christ is and on our responsibilities to him?

God is interested in your having a Christian family, but there are ground rules to be followed. Dr. Howard Hendricks states that a Christian home is not just a place where Christians live, or where middle-class standards exist, or even a place where certain practices are performed. And it is certainly not a house where perfection is exhibited. But a Christian home is typified by the proper relationships. A Christian home is centered around the Word of God. The Bible is received, believed, lived, and shared. Each person of the home has a relationship with Christ and with the Bible. The person of Christ is also received and shared on a daily basis. And, of course, the will of God is also received, believed, and shared in a truly Christian home.

God has said that there cannot be a Christian home, and the Christian cannot be in his will, unless both marriage partners are truly born-again believers and are in a proper relationship with him.

Believers have been re-created in order to honor God. Disobedience to his Word does not honor him. An unequally yoked marriage obligates the Christian to a child of Satan. A Christian wife is under obligation to obey and seek to please her husband. The Christian husband must love, nurture, and admonish his wife. However, if either partner is trying to obey his scriptural role in marriage toward an unsaved partner, the problems are immense. Anyone who tries to live up to God's standards for a husband or wife knows that it is a difficult task indeed. When the task is complicated by one partner who does not understand and receive the biblical standards, the problems are many.

The believing partner will want to raise his children to honor God. The unbelieving partner will give his children an excuse not to believe. The unsaved husband never has to tell his son that Christianity is for women. He just raises his son in a home where the wife is the stronger person spiritually.

A mixed marriage is likely to be a battleground for religion, and children will naturally retreat from such battlegrounds.

There is no way possible in this universe that God will ever give permission for a Christian to marry a non-Christian. God has spoken on this issue and he has not stuttered. The Christian who wants God's will concerning his future partner will choose that partner very carefully, and according to God's Word.

DISCUSSION QUESTIONS

1. Why is it impractical, as well as unscriptural, for a Christian to marry a non-Christian?

2. What are some of the problems faced in a spiritually mixed marriage?

3. What should a Christian who is now married to a non-Christian do to witness to his/her mate? Be very practical here.

4. Can you distinguish between love and infatuation? How?

5. List the nine items on pages 49, 50 in order of priority for you. This is a personal matter, so your list may differ from someone else's. Discuss the differences.

SUGGESTED READING

Design for Christian Marriage, Dwight Small. Fleming H. Revell, 1952.
Dating, Clyde M. Narramore. Zondervan, 1974.
For You, Teen-Ager in Love, Walter Riess. Concordia, 1965.

God's Will and Your Sex Life

 Most people assume that "God's will for your life" is limited to our religious doings; that God is only interested in how often we attend Sunday school, read the Bible, and pray.

But God speaks plainly on all matters, including the tough job of raising children and getting along with your husband or wife. Even when it comes to the Christian home, some still limit God's Word and God's will to religious things. But God is concerned about our entire lives, including our sex life.

In 1 Thessalonians 4:1-3, Paul stresses the importance of the matter: "You already know how to please God in your daily living, for you know the commands we gave you from the Lord Jesus himself. Now we beg you—yes, we demand of you in the name of the Lord Jesus—that you live more and more closely to that ideal. For God wants you to be holy and pure, and to keep clear of all sexual sin."

Notice the words "commands," "beg," and "demand." The Greek word translated "commands" referred to strict military orders.

Paul explained to the Thessalonians, and to us, that a

better understanding should provide a better walk. But we should also be aware that this subject is for the mature. The Thessalonian Christians were already walking and abounding in the Spirit. They were mature believers.

Yesterday's Christians hid their heads when sex was mentioned. But that can no longer be the position of a Christian. The shades are up in our society. Today's best-sellers were yesterday's pornography. Now we can speak more openly to college students than to adults about sex.

Mature Christians today realize that sex is a God-given drive, and it is nothing of which to be ashamed. God created the human race male and female. Sexual difference was God's idea. God gave a whole book of the Bible to the subject of a love poem (including sex) when he wrote the Song of Solomon.

But the mature Christian will also realize that the human species has perverted and prostituted sex. Segments of our society claim we are in a sex revolution. The excuse used most often to justify our sex-saturated society is that people have been warped concerning sex because the subject has traditionally been hushed up. But a look at the last twenty years reveals that sex has had its say and people are still warped on the subject. All the free talk about it really hasn't helped.

The natural appetite for sex has been twisted. C. S. Lewis compares the situation to someone who notices that people are pouring into a dimly lit room. There is an air of seductiveness as the band plays and the spotlight focuses on a covered object on the stage. Then someone carefully, but slowly, uncovers the object. And there it is—a lambchop! As one drives down the highway, he sees lambchops displayed on billboards, cars, hotels. The world has taken a natural appetite for lambchops and gone crazy. Well, that's about what has happened to the God-given sex drive.

Sex is an important part of life. But it should not control life. God did create our first parents as male and female, but that's not all they were. Sex was created for the enjoyment and procreation of the race. But just as appetites for food, drink, and sleep have boundaries and limitations, so does the drive for sex. "For God wants you to be holy and pure, and to keep clear of all sexual sin" (1 Thessalonians 4:3).

The phrase "sexual sin" includes all sexual immorality. It encompasses more than adultery. Limitations are God's will. Some teen-agers or married people risk immorality even though they fear their parents, the police, or pregnancy. Yet it is God who should be most feared. He sees that act. He is there for every immoral move.

God places limitations on your sex life for your own spiritual welfare. Satan doesn't tell us, "Follow me and I'll destroy your life." He simply whispers in our ear, "Have a little fun; everyone is doing it; no one will find out; isn't this drive given to you by God?"

Probably most Christians who disobey this limitation don't really intend to do so—at the beginning. Teen-agers on a date don't plan to end up in a sea of guilt, shame, and trouble with their parents. Married people who flirt with the opposite sex don't intend to be involved in the disgrace of adultery. But these things happen when one ignores God's limitations.

There is a parallel truth in 1 Corinthians 6:18—"run from sex sin." 1 Thessalonians 4:4 tells the married Christian how to keep sex sins out of his marriage. Just as there are limitations, there are obligations.

I like the way Williams translates verses 3, 4: "For it is God's will that you should keep pure in person, that you should practice abstinence from sexual immorality, that each man among you should learn to take his own wife out of pure and honorable motives, not out of evil passions."

The King James uses the word "vessel," also used in 1 Peter 3:7. "Vessel" is a clear reference to one's own wife.

When a husband (or a wife) comes to the marriage bed, he (or she) should come undefiled to possess the marriage partner. But this presupposes a problem Paul deals with in 1 Corinthians 7:3, 4. The vessel must be available: "The man should give his wife all that is her right as a married woman, and the wife should do the same for her husband: for a girl who marries no longer has full right to her own body, for her husband then has his rights to it, too; and in the same way the husband no longer has full right to his own body, for it belongs also to his wife."

According to these verses, the sexual relationship in marriage is not a favor but a debt. It is not being spiritual to abstain from normal sex relations with your marriage partner.

The debt should be paid willingly, not just when the emotion strikes you. Yes, the debt should even be paid when you are tired. You may need to rearrange your schedule so that you will not be so tired at night. Put the payment of this debt on the top of your priority list. I didn't write that. God did.

Excuses for not fulfilling one's obligation are often because of fear—fear of not satisfying the partner, fear of conception, etc. All couples must realize that such adjustments take time; such fears can be overcome.

To be sure, there is an exception for payment of the debt. "The only exception to this rule would be the agreement of both husband and wife to refrain from the rights of marriage for a limited time, so that they can give themselves more completely to prayer. Afterwards, they should come together again so that Satan won't be able to tempt them because of their lack of self-control."

Be sure all three conditions are met—the agreement must be mutual; it must be temporary; the purpose must be spiritual.

But what about a wife with a cruel husband who unreasonably demands payment of the debt? God discusses that problem also. First Thessalonians 4:5 says, "Not in lustful passion as the heathen do, in their ignorance of God and his ways."

The vessel should be possessed with honor, not with

lust. First Peter 3:7 says the wife is to be treated as a co-heir. The marriage bed is beautiful, and is not to be cheapened with lust. It is for this reason that a Christian marriage has deeper roots than the non-Christian marriage.

It's amazing how many Christians don't realize this truth. Frequently in counseling and in Bible studies, it becomes evident that a Christian husband has sex with his wife as though she were a prostitute. And Christian wives have sex with their husbands as though they were someone they just met in a bar. The love and intimacy, the closeness and spiritual relationship that God meant for married people is missing. The act is no more than an act of personal gratification. The act is animal behavior, not Christian love. It seems to me that true Christians ought to feel as close to God during love-making with their spouse as at any other time.

God is in favor of fun, and that surely includes the marriage bed. Techniques and creativity are not only permissible, but advisable. Yet the whole approach must have deeper roots than many Christian couples have.

Often when a man (married or unmarried) wants sexual gratification he will say to a woman, "I love you, I love you, I love you." But what he may mean is, "I love me, I love me, I want you." Love seeks the most good possible for the person loved, seeking to satisfy the other person, not yourself.

Just a word about that phrase "lustful passion." When one possesses his partner with passions of lust and seeks to satisfy himself rather than his partner, that person is in danger of becoming an unfaithful partner. When another comes along who will be able to satisfy that lust more fully, then temptation may overcome him (or her). But if the relationship with your partner is one of true love, the waves of temptation will not be able to wash you from your moorings.

Unfaithfulness to your partner makes you unclean before God (1 Thessalonians 4:7). Temple prostitutes were available to the Thessalonians in Paul's day, and every man in every office has plenty of opportunities today. But even if everyone else seems to be doing it, it will make you unclean and uncomfortable before God.

Unfaithfulness to your partner reveals your relationship with God (see verse eight). Remember that your body is the home of the Holy Spirit (1 Corinthians 6:19). In the context, that verse is sandwiched between the one which says "run from sex sin" (6:18) and the ones which speak of paying your sexual debts to your partner (7:3-5). The primary meaning then of your body being the home of the Holy Spirit is to keep yourself sexually clean.

One of the supporting beams under the foundation of America is the home. It is obvious to all observers that this beam is disintegrating to a dangerous extent. One of the chief culprits of this decay is unfaithfulness. God speaks frankly in this passage when he says that you can help head off unfaithfulness in your marriage by observing these rules:

1. Obey the limitations; flee sex sin.
2. Obey the obligations; possess your partner with honor, not with lust; pay your debts to your partner.
3. Obey the admonitions; obey God carefully.

And remember that these words are from God—God's will for your life includes your sex life.

DISCUSSION QUESTIONS

1. Why is the Bible so blunt about the matter of sex?

2. How does one possess his partner in sanctification in the sex relationship? How should the sex relationship of a Christian husband and wife differ from the relationship in a non-Christian marriage?

3. What are the motivations for a Christian married person to limit his sexual relationships to his own partner?

4. What are the sexual obligations of a Christian toward his partner? What are the exceptions? How often should exceptions be granted?

5. What are some of the major causes of unfaithfulness in marriage?

SUGGESTED READING

Sex without Fear, Norman Applezweig. Medical Research Press, 1967.

The Joy of Sex, Alex Comfort (Editor). Crown, 1972. (Morality of the book not endorsed; for married people only.)

Sexual Happiness in Marriage, Herbert J. Miles. Zondervan, 1967.

How to Tell Your Children about Sex, Clyde M. Narramore. Zondervan, 1973.

God's Will and
Your Marriage

"Be filled instead with the Holy Spirit." That's God's will for your life, insists the Apostle Paul in Ephesians 5:18. Just three verses later, he turns to the subject of family relationships. It's one thing to be filled with the Spirit while at church reading psalms and singing hymns (Ephesians 5:19, 20), but it is quite another matter to be filled with the Spirit while arguing with your mate or spanking your children.

Paul discusses the relationship of wives to husbands, children to parents. He seems to be saying that the results of a Spirit-filled life will be evident in the marriage relationship.

Our society often jokes about marriage, and the innocent (?) jokes often rub off on the younger generation. A friend tells of her seven-year-old neighbor who had just seen a movie about Cinderella. The child was testing the lady's knowledge of the fairy tale. The neighbor, anxious to impress the little girl, said, "I know what happens at the end." "What?" asked the child. "Cinderella and the Prince live happily ever after." "No, they didn't," announced the little girl, "they got married." I am not sure that this is the attitude we wish our children to carry to the wedding altar, but evidently many do. Some statistics show that one in every three marriages now end in divorce.

But divorce is only part of the picture. Thousands of married couples exist in armed truce. They don't seek a divorce, because of the children, social or religious pressures, or Christian convictions. They simply live in holy deadlock.

From my observations, I believe that the real problem of the home is not that the wife spends too much money, or that the husband is a bore. The basic problem isn't that the wife nags, or that the husband spends too little time at home.

The real problem is that the basic pattern outlined in Scripture is ignored. The Bible really does have something to say about God's will and your marriage. Let it be clearly understood that the Bible speaks and gives counsel only to the Christian. The one who is not yet a believer in Jesus Christ must put first priority on coming to know the Savior. Only then can an individual live a Spirit-filled life which will help his marriage relationship.

The Spirit-filled wife will be in subjection to her husband. Subjection is a mark of spirituality. "You wives must submit yourselves to your husbands' leadership in the same way you submit to the Lord" (Ephesians 5:22). Subjection of women is certainly unpopular today. The equality of the sexes is stressed everywhere. This verse rubs some women the wrong way. One recent poll showed that ninety percent of all brides don't want the word "obey" in their marriage vows. It's possible to erase words from marriage vows, but one can't erase Scripture.

Subjection is often misunderstood. Subjection is not suggested here because of a basic inferiority of women. The issue is a matter of spirituality. The woman who is not submissive to her husband is not a spiritual wife.

Subjection is a recognition of divine order. "For a husband is in charge of his wife in the same way Christ is in charge of his body the church" (Ephesians 5:23). Subjection is by position, not person. Paul explains that subjection is because of the order of creation (1 Corinthians 11:8-12).

We know that subjection is a necessary part of life. When three men form a partnership and create a new company, they must divide their responsibilities. One will become president, another treasurer, and perhaps the third will be manager of production. Obviously, not all can be president. The family must also have a division of responsibility. Paul was emphatic in saying that women should be in subjection to their own husbands (Ephesians 5:24). Wives are not to be in subjection to husbands as a class. Their responsibility is to their own husband.

Subjection is to be entered into willingly. No wife who grits her teeth while being in subjection is in God's will. Ephesians 5 shows that a wife should be as willing to obey her husband as the church is to obey Christ.

No woman is happy as the head of her home. It is not a compliment to tell a Christian wife that she is running things. That surely embarrasses her before her husband, before others, and before God.

Subjection extends to all areas of life. "So you wives must willingly obey your husbands in everything, just as the church obeys Christ" (Ephesians 5:24). The principle is valid. The wife is to be in subjection to her husband in all things. The Bible is clear on the issue.

Of course, problems do remain. Should a Christian wife obey her unsaved husband? Another scriptural principle teaches that we should obey God rather than man. Every Christian woman who is married to a non-Christian and is seeking God's will for her life strives for a balance, and compromises with her husband (but not with God) in order to win him. (Read 1 Peter 3:1-6.) Perhaps the unsaved husband believes that three times a week at church is too often. The wise Christian wife will stay home from church at certain times in order to be a good testimony to her unsaved husband. One partner not fulfilling his obligations does not release the other partner from his (or her) scriptural duties.

The Christian wife seeking God's will must also obey a Christian husband who may be out of fellowship with God. Even if the husband will not take the lead and fulfill his obligations in the marriage, the Christian wife will continue to seek to obey God's Word. The wise wife will not club her husband with her spirituality. She will not nag him. She will be patient. That's difficult, but it is possible.

The old saying is that "behind every great man there stands a woman." Now there is some truth in that. Yet the Bible emphasizes just the opposite in the Christian marriage.

The Spirit-filled husband will love his wife. Love provides for the wife's spiritual needs. "And you husbands, show the same kind of love to your wives as Christ showed to the church when he died for her" (Ephesians 5:25). Because of the previous verses in this chapter, some have felt that Paul taught that marriage is for the gratification of the man only. That is not true. The man is to be the leader, but he has no right to lead in the wrong way. The Christian husband loves his wife and sees her as an individual, not a thing.

This kind of love always causes a response. It is not hard for a woman to be in submission to a man who loves her as Christ loved the church. Remember that Christ loved the church not because it was perfectly lovable, but in order to make it so. Christian husbands seeking God's will should not berate their wives for lack of submission; they should love their wives as Christ loved the church.

Love always sanctifies (Ephesians 5:26, 27). The daily duty of the husband is to lead his wife in spiritual matters. He is to make her holy before God. This is not accomplished by giving her things, but by leading her in the way in which she should go.

There are long-range goals also, as Paul shows in

Ephesians 5:27. A contemporary *Reader's Digest* article makes the point:[1]

> Some things don't improve with age. Wives are an exception. The longer they are married, the better, as a rule, they become.
>
> A ten-year-old automobile is ready for the junk pile. Its glass is gone, it creaks and squeaks, its performance is faulty and it costs too much to have it overhauled.
>
> Some men think wives are like that. Since it is illegal to throw a wife on a junk pile, they dispose of her in some more orderly manner and get a new model.
>
> But they are wrong. A wife is not like an automobile. Ten years after saying, "I do," she is just beginning to show her mettle.
>
> Every year after that she gets better and more useful to her husband. After fifteen or twenty years she may need an occasional repaint job, but she is certainly worth it. After twenty-five years a wife becomes indispensable.
>
> She may not look as glossy, but she has more under the hood. The buttons she sews on stay on longer.
>
> She may still believe that money grows on trees, but she realizes that kind of tree doesn't grow in your backyard.
>
> When she occasionally has to carry the garbage out, she doesn't make a federal case out of it.
>
> If she finds a blonde hair on your coat, she doesn't make a big scene. She knows that some woman just brushed against you on the bus.
>
> She no longer yells about going home to

[1]Hal Boyle, "What Every Husband Ought to Know," *Reader's Digest*, July 1966, p. 40 (© 1966 Associated Press).

Mother if you overdo anything. Her biggest threat is, "I'll tell your doctor on you."

The meals she fixes don't taste like a misprint in an Armenian cookbook.

If her vacuum cleaner breaks down, she fixes it herself.

In a pinch, she'll dip into her secret emergency fund and lend a husband a little extra for lunch. (You can never expect this from young wives; they're always broke).

Yes, it takes a lot of time, trouble and understanding for a husband to take a flibbertigibbety young bride and turn her into man's greatest masterpiece—a perfect wife, nobly planned.

But in what more rewarding manner can a fellow spend his years?

The spiritual husband will also provide for his wife's physical needs. "That is how husbands should treat their wives, loving them as parts of themselves. For since a man and his wife are now one, a man is really doing himself a favor and loving himself when he loves his wife! No one hates his own body but lovingly cares for it, just as Christ cares for his body the church" (Ephesians 5:28, 29).

The Christian husband seeking God's will sees his wife's needs as being as important as his own needs. He will love her in spite of her imperfections, even as he does his own body. There may be things that the husband dislikes about his wife, but he still has the responsibility to love her. The man who does not love his wife and treats her poorly does damage to his own personality. He will be out of fellowship with God because he is not obeying the Scriptures, he will lose his self-respect, and he will lose respect for his wife.

The obligation for the Christian husband extends to every area of love (Ephesians 5:29, 30). The husband is to bring his wife to maturity. Very frequently the husband enjoys intellectual pursuits at his job. He must remember that there is not a great deal of stimulation in changing diapers and wiping finger marks off the walls. He needs to provide sufficient outreach for his wife. The husband is to also provide warmth and tenderness for his wife. He should share his life with her. In every Christian marriage where the partners are filled with the Spirit, there is communication. The husband must tell his wife that he loves her—often. No marriage can long endure silence.

God commands that Christians be filled with the Spirit. When he gave an example of how to do that, he used the relationship of marriage. To the wife God directs, "Be in subjection to your husband in all things." To the husband God demands, "Love your wife, and demonstrate it in all areas of life." God rests the whole cup of commandments not on your relationship with your partner, but on your relationship with him. The Spirit-filled marriage will evidence unity. "That the husband and wife are one body is proved by the Scripture which says, 'A man must leave his father and mother when he marries, so that he can be perfectly joined to his wife, and the two shall be one.' I know this is hard to understand, but it is an illustration of the way we are parts of the body of Christ" (Ephesians 5:31, 32).

When God first told a married couple to leave their parents, there were no parents (Genesis 2:24). This must be an important principle with God. The new relationship to be established involves a husband and wife literally gluing to one another.

The summary of the matter is Ephesians 5:33, "So again I say, a man must love his wife as a part of himself; and the wife must see to it that she deeply respects her husband—obeying, praising and honoring him." The woman, who is loving by nature, is told to obey. The man, who is domineering by nature, is told to love.

Jewish scholars used to say that woman was not taken from man's head that she may rule over him, she was not taken from his feet that she should be his slave, but she was taken from his side to be a companion in life. The rib was removed from under his arm showing she should live in his protection. The woman was created from near the man's heart, so she could be the special object of his love.

The married Christian interested in God's will for his life has a Spirit-filled life which is evidenced in his marriage.

DISCUSSION QUESTIONS

1. Why did God choose the marriage relationship as a testing ground for being filled with the Spirit?

2. In very practical ways, what does a wife's subjection mean? What does it not include?

3. In very practical ways, how does a husband demonstrate love?

4. What is the best way to revive communication in a marriage when there is a communication problem?

5. Why are the analogies used in Ephesians 5 so important?

SUGGESTED READING

The Christian Family, Larry Christenson. Bethany Fellowship, 1970.
The Woman in Her Home, Ella May Miller. Moody Press, 1968.
I Am a Woman, Ella May Miller. Moody Press, 1967.
The Art of Understanding Your Mate, Cecil Osborne. Zondervan, 1970.

God's Will and
Your Children

One night as I walked the halls of the hospital where I was a chaplain, the electronic device on my belt sounded. I responded and was told that an infant had died. I met the attending physician, and we headed for the waiting room to inform the parents. The doctor told me, "There was no need for that baby to die." The parents had allowed the baby to dehydrate to the point that she did not have enough fluid in her body to close her eyelids. "It doesn't seem fair," the doctor grumbled, "that some children are born into incapable hands."

Training children (and caring for them) has never been a simple task. Evelyn Duval, a noted authority in child psychology, has pointed to parenthood as the last stronghold of the amateur. Many of the current parent-child tensions in the home are not caused by the children.

An Eastern university conducted a study on the impact made on children by various forces in our society. The study showed that thirty-one percent of the influence on a child was attributed to his peers; sixteen percent came from his school and other organizations; but fifty-three percent of the impact on his life came from his home. That's the way it is, and that's the way it ought to be.

But it takes wisdom to raise children. Surely it's the toughest job in the world and quite frankly, I've never met anyone wise enough for the position.

God gives parents the opportunity to build a life for eighteen to twenty years. How is that for an in-depth ministry? God's Word teaches that parent and child relationships involve spiritual duties.

Children have a responsibility toward their parents. "Children, obey your parents; this is the right thing to do because God has placed them in authority over you" (Ephesians 6:1). On some occasions a child may find it difficult to want to obey his parents. It may be that the child who obeys his parents will be the only kid on the block who has to endure certain restrictions or limitations imposed upon him. But the issue here is not the fairness of the situation but his obedience to God's Word. The Bible tells children to obey their parents.

The Greek word used in Ephesians 6:1 which is translated "obey" is different from the word translated "submit" in Ephesians 5:21. The emphasis of the word here is upon listening. Surely many problems would be solved in every home if children were just taught to listen.

Obeying parents is a command of God. "Honor your father and mother. This is the first of God's Ten Commandments that ends with a promise" (Ephesians 6:2). The child should remember that his parents' relationship to God never excuses him from his obedience to God. In other words, a Christian child should obey his non-Christian parents. When parents are requiring actions that are contrary to the child's Christian convictions, the child should seek advice from a mature Christian adult.

When a child disobeys his parents, when he goes places, says things, and acts in ways that would displease them, there is a chance that he can escape the eye of his mother and the hand of his father, but the Christian child or young person should remember that there is not a roof big enough to hide him from God.

LIVE
CONFIDENTLY
[70]

Obedience to one's parents also avoids punishment from God. ". . . if you honor your father and mother, yours will be a long life, full of blessing" (Ephesians 6:3). This verse, quoted from the Old Testament (Deuteronomy 5:16), gives a principle no one can afford to ignore.

By the way, according to Exodus 21:15, 17, a child who struck or cursed his parents was to be executed by stoning. Rebellious children aren't stoned today, but God does still punish them.

Disobedience many times carries its own seeds of destruction. Many teen-agers who rebel against their parents later see how this action affected their lives. Unfortunately, many of these young people (some Christians included) have marked their lives with scars that cannot be erased.

Children are responsible to obey their parents, and failure to do this will bring the wrath of God upon them. But parents also have a spiritual duty toward their children. "And now a word to you parents. Don't keep on scolding and nagging your children, making them angry and resentful. Rather, bring them up with the loving discipline the Lord himself approves, with suggestions and godly advice" (Ephesians 6:4). The burden rests upon the father's shoulders, but the mother is involved too. The Greek word *pateras* can mean both parents. The mother should be in subjection to her husband. When she isn't, she confuses the child and his relationship to both parents. United discipline is necessary. Children are born extortioners. They learn early in life which parent to ask for certain favors.

A few years ago a certain judge in New York City went to Italy to discover why so few Italian young people were delinquents. When the judge returned to the United States, he wrote an article entitled "Nine Words to Solve Delinquency." They were: "Put father back at the head of the home."

The duty of the father is to stop provoking his child to

anger. Every parent must be careful not to discipline his child when he is frustrated at another problem. When one is mad at the boss or has fought with his spouse or just doesn't feel well, he should make sure he doesn't take it out on his children.

Unfair discipline will provoke the child to anger also. Always make sure that the child understands why he is being disciplined.

The parent's failure to admit when he is wrong will cause problems in the home too. I like that Dennis the Menace cartoon that shows Dennis outwitting his Dad. Suddenly Dad yells at Dennis and orders him to leave the room immediately. As Dennis leaves, he whispers to his dog Ruff, "When he yells, that means I'm right."

The parents' spiritual duty toward their children also involves the matter of provoking discouragement (Colossians 3:21). Too much discipline may do just that. Make sure that you don't give your children unattainable goals. Some children really are not capable of making A's in school. Other children may not be capable of performing well in athletics. Don't expect too much from your child for his age. Excessive parental pressure alienates children.

Be sure that you are not overly critical of your child's fads and friends. Remember that learning is a process. The mother who called her teen-age girl's room "disorganized grime" may have been too harsh. A parent's words can rub like sandpaper on the spirit of the child.

Failure to commend may also provoke discouragement. Some parents have the attitude that when it is done right, that's the way it ought to be and nothing needs to be said. But when it's done wrong, there is complaint and criticism. Undoubtedly many Christian parents give fewer compliments to their own children than they do to the Sunday school students they teach only one hour a week.

Parents have children not to have and to hold, but to have and to mold. The duty of parents is to nurture their children. Nurture involves discipline. That means more than physical punishment. It must involve correction of the wrong act. Proper discipline will not alienate children. Oh yes, the child may feel hurt or may pout for a short time, but basically children desire discipline. Proper discipline shows love and concern on the part of the parent.

Parents have a duty to admonish their children too, with words of correction and words of advice. Always be willing to advise your children on what they hear. Be concerned about the training they get from their school, television, etc. I once met a businessman who often used dishonest ethics in order to gain more money. He explained that when he was a young child, he heard his uncle, who worked for the county, explain that he was getting kickbacks from a certain tractor company because he purchased all of the county's equipment from that company. Both his uncle and his dad thought that this was clever since it was financially profitable. This man, many years later, was still greatly influenced by that one conversation between the two adults.

Parents must be alert to recognize their own children's faults. Be careful about making too many excuses for your child. Years ago I worked with a young person who was a terror in the youth group which I led. One of his biggest problems was that his parents always defended his bad behavior to school and church authorities. That boy at one time married a girl who was already pregnant with his child. He spent time in jail, and he has wandered from job to job for many years. His life has been hurt because his parents failed to recognize his faults and teach him properly.

All parents must constantly remind themselves that nagging and yelling does not admonish the child. It only relieves the frustration of the parent, and it is certainly not good for anyone involved. Abraham Lincoln once said that the way to train up a child in the way that he should go is to travel that way first yourself.

The duties of parents toward their children are spiritual responsibilities. The parent who wants God's will for his family will be in proper relationship with God. Very frequently a child's image of God comes from the image he has of his father.

> My little boy came to me one day,
> placed his tiny hand in mine and said,
> "Daddy, what is God like?"
> And I said, "God is like love and sunshine,
> And all the good things you know."
> He smiled into my eyes and said,
> "Then, Daddy, God must be just like you."
> I remembered how Jesus said that "God is like a Father."
> And I had to bow my head in shame that I, a father, was so unlike God.

Christian parents must never forget that it is their responsibility to teach their children about God. This is not primarily the duty of the church. Even a Christian school is not to assume this duty in place of the parents. Daily Bible reading and prayer is essential in building a Christian home. As a rule, devotions for the family should be regular, interesting, varied, and brief (especially for young children). That takes effort, but it is important. Don't neglect this for your family. Find the best time for your family, and make that time top priority.

Spiritual responsibilities always require time. Parents should begin early with their children. From birth to twelve years old, responsible parents teach their children to obey. But from twelve to eighteen years of age, the parents should be in the process of teaching their children to leave home and become responsible people on their own. Very frequently I've had parents come to me at summer camps and complain that they have a fifteen-year-old child with whom they can do nothing. Often I am tempted to say, "You are beginning fifteen years too late."

Spiritual parents spend time with their children. The parent who constantly chases away his child when he is reading the newspaper will at one time in the future wish that the child would interrupt his newspaper reading and share his burdens with him. Many parents spend too much of the early years of a child's life providing things for their children that they never had, and forget to provide the things for their children that they did have.

Children have a spiritual duty to obey their parents. Obedience to one's parents avoids discipline from God. Parents have the duty to discipline their children. They must do it with a proper motive and in the right way. All parents need to spend time with their offspring and seek the wisdom from God that allows one to properly raise his family.

OUR CHILD

Each little child God sends our way
Is like a piece of soft, new clay;
'Tis ours to mold and shape and trim,
To make it pleasing unto him.
Each little thing we do or say
Makes an impression day by day,
On every growing mind and heart,
Forming a pattern from the start.
Oh, what a solemn trust is ours,
How we must guard these precious hours!
Too soon this clay will be as stone—
Our chance is gone—our child is grown!
If we but take the time to pray,
And seek God's guidance every day,
He'll give us strength and wisdom, too,
To help our child grow strong and true.

Your Children
[75]

DISCUSSION QUESTIONS

1. What are some ways your church could help in training parents to be better parents?

2. What are some of the most important scriptural principles parents should teach their children?

3. What are some common ways parents provoke their children to wrath?

4. As you evaluate your relationship to your child, are you overly critical? Too lenient? Too harsh in discipline? Forgetful about commending? Too quick to defend your children? Guilty of nagging?

5. What are some profitable ways parents should spend time with their children?

SUGGESTED READING

Heaven Help the Home, Howard Hendricks. Victor Books, 1973.
Dare to Discipline, James Dobson. Tyndale House, 1972.
Taylor's Bible Story Book, Ken Taylor. Tyndale House, 1970.
The Wonderful Difficult Years, Richard DeHahn. Victor Books, 1973.

God's Will and
Divorce and
Remarriage

We live in a secular society. There is a reaction by a vocal minority against Christian ethics and morals. More and more pressure is being pushed upon us to discourage the teaching of Christian ethics. Of course, the lack of Christian ethics simply means that another system of ethics is being substituted in its place. All men have a system of morals and ethics.

A certain school district decided it couldn't make spring break coincide with Easter, because that would be favoring a religious holiday. In some places public celebrations of Christmas cannot include hymns or manger scenes, and prayer has long since been chased from the classroom.

One recent June the students of a public high school asked me to give the invocation and benediction at their commencement. When the principal called me to confirm the invitation, he warned that I could not mention the name of Jesus in my prayer. I politely informed him that my prayers are to God and not to men, and I will not pray publicly when there are restrictions upon what I say. At the end of the conversation, he told me that I was free to pray as my convictions directed, but he did warn me that I had been informed about the restriction.

We operate under a new system in America. The new ethic is based upon experience. If you like it, do it! Pleasure is preferable to pain, life is short, do your own thing. This system teaches irresponsibility.

We also believe more and more in situation ethics. This system teaches that there are no absolutes. The end justifies the means. It is OK to lie, cheat, steal, if it is for a good cause. Many Christians are allowing themselves to be pushed into the mold of the world. Too often, Christians are not carefully evaluating what is happening. They blindly accept the standards of the hour. Dr. Gary Collins warns:

> The fact that millions of people share the same vices does not make the errors to be truths: and the fact that millions of people share the same forms of mental pathology does not make these people sane.[1]

The Bible shouts against the standards of the hour. The Bible firmly preaches absolutes. Jesus taught absolutes and explained their practical implications so we would have no trouble understanding what God meant when he said, "Thou shalt not commit adultery."

In the Sermon on the Mount, Jesus taught that adultery involves lust. "The laws of Moses said, 'You shall not commit adultery.' But I say: Anyone who even looks at a woman with lust in his eye has already committed adultery with her in his heart" (Matthew 5:27, 28).

In this section of the Sermon on the Mount, Jesus was not contradicting what Moses taught. Rather, he was showing the contrast between how the rabbis had interpreted Moses and how Moses should be properly interpreted. The rabbis had quoted the letter of the law but left out the spirit. In fact, they had many times twisted the

---

[1]Gary Collins, *Search for Reality* (Wheaton, Ill.: Key Publishers, 1969) n.p.

meaning of what Moses really taught. They made obedience a mechanical and heartless activity; they had omitted love.

Jesus is simply saying in this section of his sermon that adultery (both the act and the lustful desire) is wrong. Although many would adhere to this absolute of the Scriptures, the National Center for Health Statistics announces that one-third of all of the firstborn children in America are conceived before marriage. The Alfred Kinsey Foundation reveals that sixty percent of American married men and forty percent of American married women have engaged in extramarital sexual relationships. Morton Hunt says:

> The most common attitude toward the extramarital affair is somewhat like the American attitude toward paying one's income tax: many people cheat—some a little, some a lot; most who don't would like to, but are afraid; neither the actual or the would-be cheaters admit the truth or defend their views except to a few confidants; and practically all of them teach their children the accepted, traditional code though they know they neither believe in it themselves or expect that their children will do so when they grow up.[2]

Furthermore, the Commission on Population Growth and the American Future conducted studies led by Zelnik and Kartner which showed that fifty percent of American single girls lose their virginity before twenty years of age. Fourteen percent of the fifteen-year-old girls in America have had sexual relationship. Forty-six percent of the nineteen-year-old, single American girls have had sexual relations.

---

[2]Morton Hunt, *The Affair: A Portrait of Extramarital Love in America* (New York: New American Library, 1973). n.p.

Divorce and Remarriage
[79]

God must judge that. Adultery is wrong. It is always wrong. God says so. We have forgotten the sinfulness of sin. It was sin, remember, that sent Jesus to the cross. Sin destroys relationships, people, the earth, and all that is beautiful.

But we need to understand that according to Jesus in Matthew 5, adultery begins with lust. In this same passage Jesus shows that the cure for lust may require drastic action. He uses the analogy of cutting off one's hand or plucking out one's own eye. Perhaps that drastic action to avoid lust and eventual adultery will mean changing jobs, homes, friends, or stopping dozens of times every day and asking for God's help.

The cure for lust also requires taking positive action. You can do God's will in this area of your life by removing the source of lust. Also, you must restrain the flesh and continually realize the cost of sin—for you, and for Jesus Christ. The last suggestion is to simply get started.

"You shall not commit adultery"—ever, for any reason, under any circumstances. That also means don't lust. But this law of God is attached to another truth. Often we miss the point that Jesus' teaching about divorce and remarriage was attached to his teaching about adultery.

Divorce, of course, is very common in our land. The Bureau of Census shows that divorces are up eighty percent in the last ten years. The peak divorce rate has for many years been between the first and third years after the wedding. However, we are now seeing a secondary high point. This occurs between the twentieth and thirtieth years after the wedding. The rate of divorce is up twenty-eight percent among marriages of twenty to twenty-four years of duration, and thirty-six percent among marriages which have lasted twenty-five to twenty-nine years.

God's intent in this matter is very clear—one man for one woman. Genesis 2:24 teaches that principle. The principle is repeated several times throughout the Bible. Marriage is exclusive—one man for one woman. And marriage is to be publicly recognized. Both bride and groom are to leave their parents. And marriage should be permanent. The husband is to cleave to his wife. Jesus said in his comment on this verse in Matthew 19:6 that what God has joined together, let no man put asunder. Lastly, Genesis 2:24 shows that marriage should be consummated by sexual relations.

It is true that the Mosaic Law allowd for divorce. "When a man hath taken a wife, and married her, and it come to pass that she find no favor in his eyes, because he hath found some uncleanness in her: then let him write her a bill of divorcement, and give it in her hand, and send her out of his house. And when she is departed out of his house, she may go and be another man's wife" (Deuteronomy 24:1, 2, KJV).

On one occasion Jesus was asked if he was contradicting Moses. In Matthew 19:8 he clearly showed that God allowed divorce because of the hardness of the Jewish people's hearts in Moses' day.

Moses' words in Deuteronomy 24 were not given to encourage divorce. Rather, those laws were given to slow down the process. Under these new laws, the husband had to write a formal bill of divorcement. The whole point of what Moses said was to bring order to the society and protect women from being indiscriminately put away.

From Moses to Jesus things got worse. The Greeks believed that wives were no better than slaves and had no rights. They could be divorced for any petty reason. Yet wives were expected to be faithful in all things. Husbands were not faithful. In fact, their religion allowed sexual immorality.

The Pharisees unfortunately accepted the standards of their society. They allowed men to divorce their wives for almost any reason, but wives couldn't initiate divorce against their husbands. Rabbi Shammai taught that divorce was allowed when the wife's action approached adultery. Rabbi Hillel taught that divorce was allowed for anything the wife did to displease her husband. And the fighting Rabbi Akiba said that a husband could divorce his wife when he found a more desirable wife.

The Pharisees in Jesus' day required the Jewish man divorcing his wife to write a bill of divorcement. They accepted the letter of the Mosaic Law, but they missed its intent. That is what Jesus was teaching in Matthew 5.

The Romans also allowed divorce for petty reasons. But by the first century, a wife could initiate a divorce under Roman law. There were many divorces in the society in which Jesus lived.

Jesus interpreted Moses and clarified God's will about the matter. For one thing, we must understand that Jesus never commanded divorce, but divorce was permitted in the case of fornication. "But I say that a man who divorces his wife, except for fornication, causes her to commit adultery if she marries again. And he who marries her commits adultery" (Matthew 5:32).

The word "fornication" is a broader term than the word "adultery." "Fornication" mean any sexual activity outside marriage, and evidently includes homosexuality as well as adultery.

When divorce occurs for any reason other than fornication, the one-flesh bond is still in effect. This was Jesus' point in Matthew 19. Unless fornication or remarriage occurs on the part of one party, the other party cannot remarry without committing adultery. The one who marries one who is divorced without reason of fornication, whose former mate has not committed fornication or remarried since the divorce, also commits adultery to marry such a person. When fornication or remarriage has occurred, the one-flesh bond is broken and the other person is free to remarry.

The Apostle Paul faced some new issues in 1 Corinthians 7. He taught that neither marriage or staying single is more spiritual than the other. If one is married to an unbeliever, he should stay married, Paul taught. If the unbeliever deserts and divorces the Christian, the Christian has the privilege of remarriage (verse 15). But Paul is clear (verse 39; also see 2 Corinthians 6:14-18) in saying that marriage and remarriage for the Christian can only be to another Christian. (See Chapter 3 of this book.)

Here is a summary of the Bible's teaching concerning divorce and remarriage:

1. *Divorce is never commanded.* Genesis 2:24 shows God's original intent. There always is a better way than divorce. This is a very practical problem for me as a pastor. Many times people see other counselors and pastors in our city before coming to me. Frequently I discover that people have been given the same advice by five or six counselors—get a divorce. When they come to me, I say, "No, there is a better way." I realize that sometimes so much hurt has been suffered that the individual, from his point of view, cannot restrain and must get a divorce. If one decides that he must get a divorce, I continue to counsel and help him as best I can, even though I may think that he is making a mistake.

2. *Marriage can be scripturally broken for these reasons:*
   a. Fornication, Matthew 5:32
   b. Desertion of Christian by non-Christian, 1 Corinthians 7:15
   c. Death, 1 Corinthians 7:39

3. *Remarriage can scripturally occur for these reasons:*
   a. One's mate died, 1 Corinthians 7:39
   b. One's mate committed fornication and divorce occurred, Matthew 5:32
   c. A divorce occurred and the former mate remarried, Matthew 5:32
   d. The unbelieving mate deserted and divorced the Christian, 1 Corinthians 7:15

There are some related principles which always seem to occur in a discussion such as this. For example, all breaking of God's rules before salvation are forgiven (2 Corinthians 5:17). Another issue that frequently bothers those in the church is the matter of divorced people serving in the church. The 1 Timothy 3:2 passage does not seem to prohibit one from Christian service who has been scripturally divorced or remarried. This passage either speaks about those who did not follow the scriptural pattern, or perhaps is entirely directed against the practice of polygamy which was common in Paul's day.

The principles of love, forgiveness, unity, peace, and obedience must prevail in all matters in the Body of Christ. Christians must not possess a self-righteous attitude toward those Christians who have suffered the hurt of divorce.

There seem to be several reasons why there are so many divorces in our society. Legislation is a factor. When his lawyer told one divorce-seeking husband of the "cooling-off period," the reconciliation efforts, and the child-custody investigations that are part of a Wisconsin divorce, the would-be divorcee sighed, "Forget it, I can't stay mad that long." That's exactly the point. In most of our states, we do need tougher divorce laws. In the state in which I reside, one person can get a divorce for any reason that he wishes. He really doesn't need any grounds other than the fact that he wants a divorce. In this state, divorces are always granted when only one party wants the dissolution of the marriage. Certainly there would be fewer divorces if there was forced counseling to try to keep marriages and families together.

The changing attitude toward divorce is another reason for its frequency in our society and even in the church. It is more accepted socially today than ever before. But the Christian should remember that although he does not accept divorce more readily, he still needs to show love toward the divorcee. Another reason for the rapid increase in divorces must be the desperate search for happiness without responsibility on the part of many people.

God's will for your life is that you understand adultery. Have no part of it. But if you have been caught in that sin, go from where you are. Confess the sin. God will forgive, and you can live a fruitful life for him. Other than the obvious meaning of the command, Jesus taught us that we are not even to lust, and we are not to get a divorce.

May God help each one seeking his will to live a pure life and to have a godly home.

DISCUSSION QUESTIONS

1. What is the difference between situation ethics, or the new morality, and the teaching of the Bible?

2. What are evidences of the "sexual revolution" and loosened morality in your community?

3. How does your church view divorce? May a divorced person teach in your church? Hold office? Is there room for discussion on the issue?

4. What are some ways we could reduce the number of divorces in our land? In our churches?

5. When, in your opinion, should a person get a divorce?

SUGGESTED READING

Marriage and Divorce, M. R. DeHahn. Radio Bible Class (booklet).
Divorce Problem, C. S. Lovett. Personal Christianity, 1964.
An Open Book to the Christian Divorcee, Roger Crook. Broadman, 1974.

God's Will and
Your Wallet

Oh, oh! Satan is about to attack Mr. Christian. He hits him in the foot with a poison dart. No problem! His feet are shod with the preparation of the gospel of peace. Satan's next fiery dart hits the believer in the middle section of his body. But praise the Lord, his loins are girded about with truth. Satan aims at the chest now. But no harm is done because Mr. Christian is wearing the breastplate of righteousness.

Satan keeps throwing, but each dart is knocked away by the shield of faith. Uh oh. One gets past the shield and is traveling toward the Christian's head. But the helmet of salvation keeps him safe.

It looks like Satan is defeated, or is he? Suddenly the enemy hits the Christian in his back pocket, right in the wallet. And the Christian is falling.

Art Linkletter used to say, "People are funny, especially about money." Certainly Christians are no exception to those statements. You may have already guessed that this chapter is about money, and you are looking for more pleasant pastures in another chapter. But I make no apology for teaching what the Scriptures say about the very important topic of giving.

My only request is that you give the Scriptures a fair hearing before you reach a conclusion on the matter. After all, the real issue is not what I teach or whether or not we agree. The only valid issue for one who is seeking God's will is simply, "What does the Bible say?" And regardless of your conclusion on giving, I hope that you will be honest enough to admit that God's will does extend to your wallet.

I would like to survey the Bible to summarize the truth of this topic. It is an important subject, and here it is that many Christians fall in defeat to the adversary of their souls.

The first family. The most common objection to the teaching of giving is that the tenth or tithe was God's Word under the Mosaic Law. And it is freely admitted that we are not under the obligation of that economy. But the Bible demonstrates that giving ten percent antedates the Law. In fact, some attribute tithing to the first family on this planet.

In Genesis 4 we read the story of the offering of Cain and his brother, Abel. We know that Cain's offering was not acceptable because it was not the proper kind of offering. The sin offering had to be a blood sacrifice, and his was not. The divine commentary on this event is found in Hebrews 11:4: "By faith Abel offered unto God a more excellent sacrifice than Cain." But the interesting word in the verse, "excellent," can also be translated "abundant." In fact, that is its primary meaning. Not only was Cain's offering not the right kind. It was not the right proportion!

Abraham. One of the best known pictures of tithing before the Law is painted in Genesis 14. There we have the beautiful type of Christ, Melchizedek, approaching Abraham, and the man of faith honoring the King of Salem with his tithes. Remember now, this is 500 years before the Law of Sinai.

Jacob. In Genesis 28 tithing is presented as the norm of giving. The background of the story shows that aged Isaac blessed Jacob and sent him to Uncle Laban to find a wife. On his first night of the journey, Jacob camped out beneath the stars with a rock for his pillow. That night he had his famous dream of the ladder. And that night God reaffirmed the Abrahamic Covenant to him. The next morning as Jacob arose, he remembered the dream and made a vow. He asked God to keep his salvation sure, provide him with enough food to eat, and provide clothes to wear. Jacob vowed that if God would supply these basic needs, then he would tithe of all his worldly possessions.

For a Christian to say, "I don't tithe because tithing was under the Law," is plainly not to understand Scripture. Tithing was before the Law. Tithing, giving a tenth of your income to God, began long before the Mosaic Law.

The law. Now it is also true that tithing was included in the Law. According to Leviticus 27:30, every Israelite was required to bring the first tithe: "A tenth of the produce of the land, whether grain or fruit, is the Lord's, and is holy." That was the law. Ten percent of the gross. No exceptions.

According to Deuteronomy, there was a second tithe. This tithe was always presented in one place, the sanctuary. It was always presented as an act of worship. In addition to this second tithe, there were provisions for a "free will offering." On years one, two, four and five of the seven-year cycle, this tithe was eaten as part of the feast days. But on years three and six, this tithe was given to the poor. On the seventh year, the land was not harvested.

Please notice that God's requirements under the Law were really much more than ten percent. Under the Law the Word was, "Do and I shall bless." Now under the New Covenant, the new economy, the Word is, "Now that I have blessed, do."

The right attitude. But even under the Law, tithing was to be accomplished with the proper attitude. In Amos we read of the imminent capture of the Jews by the Assyrians. In the fourth chapter, Amos of Tekoa tells the people to go on tithing though it wouldn't do any good. Their attitude was wrong, and tithing was only being used as an insurance policy against defeat. With that kind of an attitude, says Amos, your tithes are accomplishing zero.

We too often convey the wrong attitude in connection with tithing. The Bible does not teach that the believer is only responsible for ten percent of his income. The attitude and teaching of Scripture is not ten percent for God and ninety percent for the believer. Nowhere does Holy Writ suggest that the saint can use the remaining ninety percent as his carnal nature directs. Rather, the attitude is to be, "All belongs to God, and a tithe is the minimum I immediately return to him." We do not tithe so that God will bless and give us more. We tithe because God has already given so much and we love him and wish to follow his will.

Connected with blessing. In the well-known tithing text, Malachi 3, it is important to notice that tithing is inseparably connected with blessing. " 'Though you have scorned my laws from earliest time, yet you may still return to me,' says the Lord of Hosts. 'Come and I will forgive you.' But you say, 'We have never even gone away' " (3:7).

And then follows the famous sermon on man robbing God.

The Gospels. Tithing was introduced before the Law and included in the Law. As we turn from Malachi to Matthew, we discover that the Mosiac Law is not nullified but fulfilled. So now, as a New Testament believer, I do not obey the Ten Commandments because they appear in Exodus 20. Rather, I obey them because they are repeated in the New Testament (with the exception of the Sabbath).

Tithing is endorsed by the New Testament. The first one in the New Testament to speak on the subject was Jesus Christ. In Matthew 23 he made it clear that the tithe was considered to be the minimum: "Yes, woe upon you, Pharisees, and you other religious leaders—hypocrites! For you tithe down to the last mint leaf in your garden, but ignore the important things—justice and mercy and faith. Yes, you should tithe, but you shouldn't leave the more important things undone" (verse 23).

In no instance do we discover that the New Testament reduces an obligation imposed upon the believer by the Old Testament. The Old Testament said, "Don't kill." The New Testament command was, "Don't even hate, that is just as bad." The Old Testament said, "Don't commit adultery." The New Testament exhortation was, "Don't even lust." The Old Testament said that a tithe is required. The New Testament said the tithe is just the minimum. Jesus even told one man to sell *all* that he had. The story of the widow's offering also demonstrates that the tithe is just the minimum, the beginning.

The apostles. There is evidence that the apostles tithed. All of them were Jews, and they were accustomed to giving a tenth of their income. In the early chapters of Acts, we notice that once again the tithe is just the beginning of giving. In the church at Jerusalem, the believers sold their goods and pooled their resources. Barnabas and the others sold their property and gave the revenue to the Lord's work. There is also evidence that there were special offerings. Paul invited the Galatian churches and the Corinthian church to collect special offerings for the saints in need in other churches.

In 1 Corinthians 16:1, 2 Paul explains Christian giving. Here he is speaking primarily of a special offering, but the principles certainly apply to all New Testament giving. "On every Lord's Day each of you should put aside something from what you have earned during the week, and use it for this offering. The amount depends on how much the Lord has helped you earn."

The principles are evident:

1. Giving is to be regular. The basis of giving is not an emotional appeal of a hungry child or a sad story. We are to give regularly.
2. Giving is to be systematic. The tithe is from the gross income, and special offerings are beyond that, according to your capacity. That is required of every believer.
3. Giving is to be practiced by every believer. Paul makes a point to say "each of you." Someone has noted that even if everyone in the church were having to live at poverty level, but still faithfully tithed, the church would be adequately supported.

Faith. Tithing is a matter of faith. You may think you can't afford to tithe, but you must begin by faith. There will always be the added burden or the unexpected bill to hinder you from tithing. Satan will see to that. But the Bible teaches that any believer who is interested in God's best for his life cannot afford not to tithe.

Paul also writes: "But remember this—if you give little, you will get little. A farmer who plants just a few seeds will get only a small crop, but if he plants much, he will reap much. Every one must make up his own mind as to how much he should give. Don't force anyone to give more than he really wants to, for cheerful givers are the ones God prizes" (2 Corinthians 9:6, 7).

A spiritual matter. The Bible's doctrine of giving is tithing as a minimum. Of course, not all believers tithe. But you can tell by a casual observation, usually, who obeys God's Word in the matter of giving. Notice who attends the workday at church or who prays for the missionaries.

Notice who is really growing in Christ. They are usually the people who also give regularly.

Tithing is a spiritual matter. Some Christians give twenty-five percent of their income to the Lord's work. Many give fifteen to twenty percent. Some only give ten percent but are attempting to raise that percentage each year. And, as you might guess, the ones who are giving the highest percentage are not always the higher income families. It would be easy to list facts and figures to demonstrate how effective and efficient the work of the local church and foreign missions could be if each one would tithe. But that is not the point of this chapter. We are speaking of God's will for your life and the spiritual blessing you are missing if you are not giving according to God's plan.

D. L. Moody was once asked if he believed in tithing. "Yes," said Moody, "as the starting point. Tithing is the kindergarten of giving." If you are now tithing, ask God to allow you to increase your giving to twelve or fifteen percent next year. Then bathe in the blessings of God.

The Christian who is living a life pleasing to God is a Christian who is tithing. If you are interested in all of God's will, then tithe. God's will extends to your wallet.

DISCUSSION QUESTIONS

1. Why is the issue of money such a problem in some Christian circles?

2. When should a Christian begin to tithe? How should he increase his giving? Where should he give?

3. Why should a Christian give to God?

4. Can you share some personal experiences of God's blessing in your life as a result of obedience in giving?

5. Discuss the following method that some Christians use as a "faith-promise" method of giving:

    1. Amount per month I gave to God's work last year

          $_____

    2. Amount per month I could increase my giving

          $_____

    3. Amount per month by faith I will ask God to allow me to give this year

          $_____

    4. Total faith-promise commitment

          $_____

SUGGESTED READING

Let Not Money Put Asunder What God Has Joined Together, Carole G. Page. Accent Books, 1974.

How to Succeed with Your Money, George Bowman. Moody Press, 1960.

Faith Promise for World Witness, Norm Lewis. Back To The Bible, 1974.

LIVE CONFIDENTLY

God's Will and
Your Church

What is the church? Ask ten different Christians and you'll probably get ten different answers.

Some define the church as a building. That means the church can be destroyed, it can become old and worn out. Roland Huntford, Scandinavian correspondent for the *Observer* (London), shows what can happen if the church is defined as a building.

> As a consequence of redevelopment in Stockholm the only Catholic church was demolished. In recompense, the municipality offered a nearby site for a new church. . . . the money was collected and all appeared to be settled. But, at the last moment the Labour Market Directorate refused permission to start building on the grounds of economic stringency. In the meantime, a levy of twenty-five percent was imposed on all luxury construction under which the proposed church was judged to fall . . . In fact at the time all

churches had been put on the list of inessential buildings whose construction was banned.[1]

Mrs. Alva Myrdal, the ecclesiastical minister at the time, said, "We are dismantling the church bit by bit and when necessary we are using economic means to do so." If the church is a building, it may indeed be dismantled "piece by piece and bit by bit."

Some define the church as a denomination. That means, of course, that the church may lose its message. Some denominations become involved so heavily in social issues that they become little more than "do good" organizations. Other denominations may fall prey to an extreme narrowness and an overemphasis on creeds to replace loving action and contact with the world. If the church is a denomination, the church can merge with unbelievers. Unfortunately, many Protestants who think that only the Roman Catholics define the church as a denominational group show by their actions that they really believe the church to be a denomination too, their denomination.

If the church is defined as an organization, the church can become meaningless, only involved in busy activity or throwing dust in the air. The church as an organization can be small and lack any impact upon society. The church as an organization can be constantly fighting and feuding with itself and never accomplish anything.

But if the church is defined as the body of Christ, the total outlook becomes much brighter. Ephesians 1:22, 23 says that God put all things under Christ's feet and gave him to be the head over the church, which is his body. Paul explains that imagery of Christ's body in 1 Corinthians 12, after spending considerable time showing the necessity of each part of the body. Paul concludes in 1 Corinthians 12:27, "All of you together are the one body

---

[1] Roland Huntford, *The New Totalitarians* (New York: Stein and Day Publishers, 1972), p. 176, 177.

of Christ." Remember that Paul was speaking not to spiritual Ephesus, but to carnal Corinth when he made the point that all Christians are part of the body, which is the church.

Also, he was writing to one local congregation. All the Christians in Corinth made up the body of Christ. Each church which consists of true Christians is the body. When the church is defined as the body of Christ, this involves a living, growing, developing organism. This means that the church can't close, it will always live. Christ promised in Matthew 16:18 that "all the powers of hell shall not prevail against it." This definition enables us to cooperate with all who are true Christians. This means that we are capable as the total body of Christ of conquering social problems and individual sins. It is sad that many true Christians still define the church as a building, a denomination, or an organization, rather than following the biblical definition. By following the biblical definition of the church, which is the body of believers in Christ, you will have a larger outlook on what can be accomplished through you and others who are genuine members of that body.

The New Testament makes it clear that the church is God's work. That is evident from looking at the pages of history. The church has endured as a witness in spite of heavy odds against it. Heretics and nonbelievers have been used throughout the ages to burn, tear down, and destroy the church; but it still stands. Satan has led others to have the true church outlawed, banned, and banished, but it still stands. The church has been persecuted and ridiculed, but it still stands. The Evil One has worked from within the church to destroy its foundations and weaken its pillars, but it still stands. The endurance of the church in the world witnesses to the fact that the church belongs to God.

Furthermore, the church's effect on the world witnesses to its divine birth and purpose. When the light in the church goes dim, a whole nation falls into despair.

Where there is a bright and glowing light in the church, the nation prospers. God blesses a nation that honors him. Remember now, we are not speaking of institutional Christianity or "churchianity." Our definition is narrow and without tolerance, just as in the Bible. We speak of the church as those who are born-again believers.

One of the greatest empires the world has ever seen was the British Empire, The United Kingdom. Britain was at one time a nation that honored God. From the British Isles went forth our modern missionary movement. From those islands came John Wesley, George Whitefield, John Knox, and Charles Haddon Spurgeon. The church was a bright light in England. But now most people there have turned from God. Only twenty-nine percent of the British people believe in God, according to a recent public opinion poll of 1093 persons. Conducted by Opinion Research Center for a religious program televised by the British Broadcasting Corporation, the BBC called it the first major survey of religious beliefs in Britain since a Gallup Poll in 1963, which indicated thirty-eight percent of the British people believed in God. In England the church has been abandoned, and England is no longer the master of the sea.

The same story is true of Germany. When the church in Germany was drowned with the waves of German rationalism, liberalism, and unbelief, the country went to the bottom. Oh, yes, the institution and buildings were still standing. There was a form of godliness, but the true church was gone. There is no other explanation for people allowing the Third Reich to murder eight million people.

First Corinthians 16 gives us some principles to help understand how we should relate to God's church.

God gives leaders to the church. 1 Corinthians 16:10 tells us how church leaders are to be respected: "If Timothy comes, make him feel at home, for he is doing the Lord's work just as I am." Timothy evidently was young and inexperienced. The Corinthian Christians were carnal and could have been hard to deal with. Paul tells them, however, not to give Timothy a difficult time. The principle seems to be here, and other places in the New Testament, that there should be respect for position in the church, not necessarily always for the person who holds that position. Paul was not recommending Timothy because he was a successful businessman or because he was wealthy, or even experienced. His recommendation came because he was in the work of the Lord. It is not the man which glorifies the work but the work which glorifies the man.

Church leaders are to be followed: "Don't let anyone despise or ignore him [because he is young], but send him back to me happy with his time among you; I am looking forward to seeing him soon, along with the others who are returning" (1 Corinthians 16:11). These Christians were told to follow the leadership of the young man Timothy. It is sometimes true that church members can be cantankerous. Phillips Brooks once rented a horse and buggy to take his wife for a ride. He said to the man, "Give me the nicest horse you have, it is for my best girl." The livery man replied, "This is my best horse. He is always willing to obey, never balks, and is anxious to please. He is gentle, reliable, eager, and untiring." Brooks listened intently to the man's great praise of the horse and then replied, "Do you suppose you could persuade him to join my church? I need some members like that."

When Clyde R. Hoey was governor of North Carolina, he visited the western part of his state and met a country pastor. The usual question about how many members there were in the church brought the response "Fifty." When the governor asked, "How many of them are active?" he got the same answer. "My," he remarked, "you must have an unusual church to have 100 percent active membership." "Well," the parson admitted, "twenty-five are active for me and twenty-five are active against me."

Apollos was also a church leader (1 Corinthians 16:12). We know that Apollos had been given leadership gifts.

This is clear from our encounter with him in Acts 18. There Apollos appeared in Ephesus. He was evidently an Old Testament saint. He wasn't clearly instructed on the gospel until Priscilla and Aquila helped him into the new dispensation. Apollos was a man of great speaking ability. He was eloquent in his presentation. Leaders are given gifts that allow them to lead.

Church leaders have the responsibility to be led by the Spirit. Paul wanted Apollos to go to Corinth, but Apollos refused (1 Corinthians 16:12). Perhaps he was afraid that the "Apollos Party" would be strengthened if he appeared. He didn't feel led of the Spirit to do what Paul asked him to do. A Christian must be careful not to tell other Christians what the Holy Spirit wants them to do. Leaders must lead but must not and cannot replace the work of the Holy Spirit in fellow Christians' lives.

In 1 Corinthians 16:13 we are told to watch, be careful, be on the lookout for the enemy. We are also told to be true to the faith, or to hold on to the right doctrine. Doctrine in the church is important. It is unfortunate that many have the idea today that if Christians agree on the method of salvation, that's enough, and doctrine is secondary. The Bible certainly teaches us differently. There is to be that striving for a constant balance, however, between narrow fellowship because of small matters of doctrine and a broad outlook which does not place the proper importance upon the teaching of the New Testament.

This verse also admonishes Christians to be men and to be strong. Satan has counterfeited the idea of manliness today. Our society teaches that one is a man who drinks like a fish, uses vile enough language to peel off the wallpaper, and has the morals of a stray alley cat. But God's idea of a man is one who is strong, spiritually and morally. God gives such men to churches to lead them.

God also gives gifts to the church. Stephanas, in verses fifteen and seventeen, was evidently such a man. He was the first one to come to Christ as Savior in Greece.

Stephanas evidently had the gift of helps. He carried news of the Corinthians to Paul at Ephesus, and he was waiting to return this letter back to his hometown.

The Bible clearly teaches that each believer has at least one spiritual gift. This, of course, does not necessarily mean an office or a position in the organized church. But each believer must discover his own ability and then use it for God's glory. Before one can properly discover his ability, he must be growing and maturing in Christ. Paul admonishes his readers to follow the example of church leaders. He evidently understood that it isn't the number of members a church has that makes it a success; it's the number who are working for the Lord.

God gives leaders to the church and gifts to each believer; then to the church as a whole he gives fellowship. There is a bond of fellowship among believers. "The churches here in Asia send you their loving greetings. Aquila and Priscilla send you their love and so do all the others who meet in their home for their church service." (1 Corinthians 16:19). These people in Asia did not even know the Corinthians, yet they felt a bond of fellowship because of their common faith. Perhaps you have had the experience of going to another church in a different city, particularly for a mid-week service, and finding a tremendous bond of fellowship with people you have never met before. There are many churches, but there is one Church.

Once I was in a prayer meeting where a lady explained that she had just come from a restaurant where a small girl about eight or nine years of age was trying to witness to her parents about her new faith in Christ. The lady did not have opportunity to talk with the family, but those of us in that prayer meeting prayed for that little girl and her parents. None of us knew them, and we would probably never meet them. Yet there was a bond of fellowship with the little girl and a desire to pray for her witness to her parents.

The practices of the church illustrate its fellowship. In

the early church there was the practice of greeting one another with a holy kiss (verse 20, KJV). This was a custom left over from Judaism. We know, of course, that men kissed men and women kissed women. This oriental custom is still practiced in some countries today. It became a part of the early Christians' worship service. It was later dropped as a practice because of the confusion it caused when so many people came to church and perhaps because misunderstanding by the unsaved made it a dangerous habit to continue. This was unfortunate, because fellowship became a missing ingredient in church meetings. Many times today people come to church but don't have biblical fellowship with one another. They sit and nod politely to one another and perhaps even shake hands, but true fellowship is missing.

The way to enjoy fellowship is to stay in time with the conductor. Dr. Bruce Waltke of Dallas Theological Seminary relates the story of his young years as a violinist in the high school orchestra. In the course of the curriculum, the orchestra was to accompany a known pianist in a concert which featured the Grieg Concerto. The orchestra always tuned up to the nasal "A" of the oboe player. The oboe player in this case was a practical joker and tuned his instrument a half step sharp. The piano played the dynamic introduction, but when the orchestra came in, the noise was unbearable. They were out of tune only a little, but they were out of fellowship a lot. Just a few church members being out of tune with God will mean that the entire body will be out of fellowship a great deal.

God in his grace gives love to the church too. "Whatever you do, do it with kindness and love" (1 Corinthians 16:14). Paul said not only should the business of the church be conducted *with* love, but *in* love. He was not just saying that everything the church does is to be accompanied with love.

Love causes us to pray for one another. And Christians should enjoy praying together. Christians should enjoy praying for one another. All too often we are guilty of not communicating this properly when we pray for each other.

Some years ago I came upon my older son, Mark, explaining the gospel to my younger son, Haddon. He wanted to tell his young brother how to take Jesus into his heart. I carefully explained to Mark that we would talk with Haddon later. I assured him that when Haddon was a little older, he too would receive Christ as Savior. "How do you know?" asked Mark. "Well," I explained, "I pray every day for Haddon just like I do for you." Mark was amazed. He had no idea that I prayed every day for him. My mistake was evident.

On one particular week I had great difficulties in my own personal life. There were several traumatic experiences, including dealing with someone who burst into the church office and went berserk. Even though it was a particularly hard week, I knew someone was praying for me because of the evident peace and power I had. On Sunday, one of the men of the church came to me and told me that he had prayed extra diligently for me that week. The Lord had shown him my needs through the love relationship that we had.

Love for the Lord Jesus brings us closer to one another. "My love to all of you, for we all belong to Christ Jesus" (1 Corinthians 16:24). Corinth was a carnal church. Paul could have ended his letter to them with a rebuke, or at least an exhortation. But he ended his letter on a note of love. Paul and the Corinthians were heart to heart because of the love that God had given through the church.

Here we see some patterns, some outlines for the church. God gives leaders and gifts to the church. He gives fellowship and love to the church. Each Christian who wants God's will must assume the task of building the church into a strong, vibrant, healthy organism. Every Christian should put his very best into God's work.

DISCUSSION QUESTIONS

1. How do you define the word "church?" What is the advantage of your definition as opposed to other possible definitions?

2. What is your commitment to your local church? Why? Are you satisified with your commitment? Do you plan to change your relationship with your church? How? When?

3. What are some practical ways you can show respect for the leaders of your church?

4. Have you discovered your spiritual gift that should be used in the body of Christ? What do you think your gift may be? What steps are you taking to discover your gift? Are you helping others discover their spiritual gifts?

5. How important is fellowship with other Christians? What are some ways your church could improve its fellowship?

SUGGESTED READING

Sharpening the Focus of the Church, Gene Getz. Moody Press, 1974.
Body Life, Ray Stedman. Regal Books, 1972.
The Church at the End of the 20th Century, Francis Schaeffer. Inter-Varsity Press, 1970.
The Greening of the Church, Findley Edge. Word Books, 1972.
Discover Your Spiritual Gift and Use It, Rick Yohn. Tyndale House, 1974.

God's Will and
Your Conduct

How should a Christian act? Probably every Christian has been concerned many times in his life about the rights and wrongs, dos and don'ts of the Christian life.

Some things are easy. We don't have any problem about whether it's all right to commit adultery, get drunk, or murder our next-door neighbor. But we do have problems with choosing or refusing wine in a restaurant, making out an expense account, or choosing recreation and amusements for the family. There are personal habits which the Bible doesn't mention per se, and we have to decide what's right and what's wrong.

One way to decide is to attempt to live under the Ten Commandments and other portions of the Old Testament Law.

The Old Testament Law is found in Exodus and Leviticus. Some divide the Mosiac Codes into three parts: 1) The moral law, i.e., the Decalogue or Ten Commandments (Exodus 20); 2) the judgments, i.e., the rules which govern man's relationship with his fellow man (these begin in Exodus 21); 3) the ceremonial laws, which instructed Israel in her habits of worship.

The Jews divided the Law into 613 total laws, 365 negatives and 248 positive ones. But a closer look will reveal that the Law was a unit; it was given and obeyed as a unit. God imposed the same judgment for breaking different parts of the Law. For example, one man was struck dead for picking up sticks on the Sabbath, breaking the moral Law. The nation disobeyed the judgment laws about letting the land rest every seventh year, so God took the seventy years all at once and sent them into captivity where many of them died. The punishment for breaking the ceremonial Law was also death, as we read about the deaths of Nadab and Abihu who did not properly offer the sacrifices.

But can a Christian take refuge in the Old Testament Law? Can we pattern our lives according to those documents? The Jerusalem Council (Acts 15) said "no." The Christian is not under the obligation of the Old Testament Law.

Romans 10:4 says Christ is the end of the Law. Second Corinthians 3 teaches that all of the law has been done away with, even the Ten Commandments. Does that mean we don't have to obey the Ten Commandments in Exodus 20? Not exactly (see Chapter 9, page 90).

So all of the Law is done away, not just the ceremonial or the judgment laws. It is all passed away and holds no grip upon us.

Romans 7 says we are dead to the Law. Does civil law try to impose its regulations on dead men? No. So the Old Testament Law cannot impose its restrictions on Christians who are dead to the Law but alive to Christ. Furthermore, the purpose of the Law was to bring men to Christ. The Law was given to show men their unworthiness and to drive them to Christ by faith. But men rejected Christ. Now God is dealing with man under a new test, a new dispensation.

The New Testament man now lives under grace, under liberty. But that doesn't mean he lives without restrictions and regulations. Yet the New Testament reveals not so much a list of no-nos as a list of principles to follow.

Although we are not under the Old Testament Law, we are accountable for our conduct. One of the chapters in the New Testament which deals with the principles guiding our conduct as Christians is Romans 14. The principles there help us make choices day by day.

The first principle is that each Christian is accountable for himself before God. "Give a warm welcome to any brother who wants to join you, even though his faith is weak. Don't criticize him for having different ideas from yours about what is right and wrong. For instance, don't argue with him about whether or not to eat meat that has been offered to idols. You may believe there is no harm in this, but the faith of others is weaker; they think it is wrong, and will go without any meat at all and eat vegetables rather than eat that kind of meat" (Romans 14:1, 2).

These verses teach us that there are different convictions. For example, in the first century, some Christians thought that it was all right to eat meat which had been offered to idols. Other Christians considered this to be partaking in heathen worship. Paul says some are weak Christians, and according to 1 Corinthians 8, they are the ones with the more sensitive conscience. But here in Romans 14, he seems to be using the word "weak" to describe one who may falter on matters of conduct.

The point is that all Christians are to be accepted. We are not to make our own personal convictions the standard for fellowship. The word "receive" (Romans 14:1, KJV) is the same word used in Romans 15:7— "Wherefore, receive ye one another, as Christ also received us to the glory of God." We are not to pass judgment on another's conduct.

"Doubtful disputations" (KJV) refers to an attitude of judging. In other words, don't be horrified if an untaught believer comes to church and doesn't hold some of the same convictions you do.

In some churches certain questions are asked when one applies for membership. Good questions deal with doctrine, the Christian life, and attitudes toward both. Whether or not one wears make-up, has a beard, attends movies, or smokes cigarettes should make no difference as far as membership is concerned. Christians should accept others without disputations.

Paul continues, "Those who think it is all right to eat such meat must not look down on those who won't. And if you are one of those who won't, don't find fault with those who do. For God has accepted them to be his children. They are God's servants, not yours. They are responsible to him, not to you. Let him tell them whether they are right or wrong. And God is able to make them do as they should.

"Some think that Christians should observe the Jewish holidays as special days to worship God, but others say it is wrong and foolish to go to all that trouble, for every day alike belongs to God. On questions of this kind everyone must decide for himself. If you have special days for worshiping the Lord, you are trying to honor him; you are doing a good thing. So is the person who eats meat that has been offered to idols; he is thankful to the Lord for it; he is doing right. And the person who won't touch such meat, he, too, is anxious to please the Lord, and is thankful" (Romans 14:3-6).

Each Christian is responsible to God. We are not to judge others who don't have our convictions (verse 3). This kind of attitude leads to a super-piousness. Verse 4 teaches us that others are not responsible to us. Please don't play the role of the Holy Spirit. Another may not be ready in his maturity to decide on the matters about which God is speaking to you.

But be sure you have some personal convictions (verse five). Never accept second-hand convictions, or expect others to do so. Some parents are concerned that their teen-agers seem to reach a point where they must decide everything for themselves. The good, old reliable word from mom and dad doesn't seem to matter much any more. That's not bad, that's good. Every teen has to go through that process of seriously evaluating the convictions of his parents, minister, and friends. Usually when he reconstructs his own set of values, however, they are very close to the ones held by his parents and church.

And by all means, test your convictions (verse six). Make sure your convictions are not just a rationalization of what you want to do. Be convinced that your convictions are from the Lord, not just from your society, culture, or even your parents.

Paul deals realistically with Christian conduct. Each is accountable for himself before God. Don't judge another because his convictions don't match yours. Be sure that your convictions are from God. The point is individual responsibility.

Verses 7-9 inform us that each Christian should make Christ Lord of his life. No Christian lives in a vacuum. Our lives do show to others. Each Christian belongs to the community of the redeemed. Jesus should be Lord over each life. If such were the case, then we would certainly save a lot of anxiety over what is right and what is wrong.

After declaring that each is responsible for himself before God and we shouldn't judge each other, Paul then writes, "You have no right to criticize your brother or look down on him. Remember, each of us will stand personally before the Judgment Seat of God. For it is written, 'As I live,' says the Lord, 'every knee shall bow to me and every tongue confess to God.' Yes, each of us will give an account of himself to God" (Romans 14:10-12).

But we still find some Christians who are busy about other Christians' business. Usually these self-appointed judges are checking lists with other Christians. They think spirituality is keeping the list of the filthy five, the nasty nine, or the dirty dozen. As long as they don't do the things on the list, they believe they are receiving an "A" in Christian conduct.

If these phony Christians would just be quiet, we could

ignore them, but almost always they are imposing their list on others, and judging those who won't keep their no-nos.

Paul also says that the stumbling block principle makes us accountable to others. Verses 16-21 explain that misuse of Christian liberty is wrong. Christians do certain things, go certain places, wear certain things because "there's nothing wrong with it," even though they are aware that others are offended. Some things may not be wrong in themselves, but they become wrong if you cause another to stumble. "Don't undo the work of God for a chunk of meat. Remember, there is nothing wrong with the meat, but it is wrong to eat it if it makes another stumble. The right thing to do is to quit eating meat or drinking wine or doing anything else that offends your brother or makes him sin" (Romans 14:20, 21).

The goal of the Christian is unity and peace. "For, after all, the important thing for us as Christians is not what we eat or drink but stirring up goodness and peace and joy from the Holy Spirit" (Romans 14:17).

In other words, don't exercise your liberty if it will cause an argument. Forego your rights in order to maintain peace among the brethren. We are to edify one another with good works, not destroy one another with doubtful actions.

The Christian is accountable for his conduct before God and before others. But he is not to be a legalist who keeps certain rules and regulations in order to gain righteousness with God. The legalist is seeking brownie points for keeping the list. And usually this is a person who imposes his list on others. The Christian is not accountable for his conduct before a legalist who makes spirituality a list of don'ts. Consider carefully if your critic is in the game of the Christian life trying to discover God's will, or if he is just sitting on the sidelines shooting at others.

There is another principle of Christian conduct. "You may know that there is nothing wrong with what you do, even from God's point of view, but keep it to yourself; don't flaunt your faith in front of others who might be hurt by it. In this situation, happy is the man who does not sin by doing what he knows is right. But anyone who believes that something he wants to do is wrong shouldn't do it. He sins if he does, for he thinks it is wrong, and so for him it *is* wrong. Anything that is done apart from what he feels is right is sin" (Romans 14:22, 23).

Each Christian is accountable for himself to himself. Each must act in a manner that will not produce guilt. The "Tucker translation" of the second half of verse twenty-two reads like this, "Blessed is the man who does not feel guilty in that thing he does."

Many people today are burdened with guilt. Guilt is self-incrimination. And guilt brings depression. Some people punish themselves for their guilt. Often those people who are "accident-prone" are people who are punishing themselves, perhaps subconsciously. Some people won't forgive themselves even after they are sure God has forgiven them for a particular sin. So these people suffer guilt and depression, to pay for their sin. Some people commit crimes or act in an unacceptable manner in such a fashion that they will be sure to be caught. Underneath they really want to be caught to pay for their guilt.

Now, these verses do not mean that a Christian should condition his conscience so that he doesn't feel guilty when he sins. Most people feel guilty because they *are* guilty. The removal of guilt is not accomplished by conditioning, but by receiving forgiveness. And that only comes when one is in a right relationship with God. These verses in Romans 14 are preventative medicine. Don't do things which will cause you to be and feel guilty. When you are burdened with guilt, you cannot function well in any area of life.

Each Christian should constantly be evaluating his own actions. Certain conduct may be lawful, but not expedient. Don't do things which will cause you to feel guilty.

What is harmless for one may be sin for another. We need to evaluate often, because we are always changing, maturing. Maybe some of the things we have not done in the past because of convictions, we will now be able to do. Perhaps some things we have been doing, we will need to omit in our lives.

You need to know how to act as a Christian. You need some principles to guide your life. Romans 14 supplies three of those principles. The first is to keep your sanctified snout out of other Christians' business. If you see a brother in sin, pray for him, don't criticize him, don't gossip about him. If his sin is affecting the testimony of the church or the testimony of other Christians, then the Bible tells us we should go to that person or ask the church leaders to go to that person and pray with him, asking him to repent. If he will not run from his sin, then we are to return with another and ask him again in the spirit of love. If he still refuses, the matter should be brought before the church, and church discipline exercised. (Matthew 18:15-17 spells this out.)

The second principle is that we must not offend another with our actions. If our behavior offends, then we must change.

The third principle is that we should not offend our own consciences and feel guilty over what we do.

Dr. Donald Grey Barnhouse once asked a mission board executive who was wise with years of experience to list the negative and positive traits which the Christian should seek most to omit and include in his life. After a considerable length of time, the following list was submitted:

NEGATIVE TRAITS TO BE AVOIDED

unforgiving spirit
self-seeking
a legalistic spirit

LIVE
CONFIDENTLY
[112]

playing God for others
hypocrisy
failing to appreciate others' gifts
failing to make allowances for one another
a lack of patience
not sympathizing with others' infirmities or
    their lack of gifts we possess
evil-speaking
assuming, without grounds, that others are at
    fault
pulling one another to pieces
suspecting the motives of others
a domineering spirit
a rebellious spirit
snobbery
hatred
grumbling
arguing
murmuring, complaining
maliciousness
being a busybody
greediness
bitterness
resentment
a sense of inferiority—not resting or relying
    on the Lord—not satisfied with the gifts he
    has given us
a lack of security
instability
timidity
spite
laziness
economic sponging
lying and slander
jealousy
thinking too highly of oneself
a critical spirit toward others
carrying on controversy

POSITIVE TRAITS TO ACQUIRE

a willingness to be in subjection
considering others better than self
an understanding spirit
a sense of intimate relationship to Christ
not insisting on our rights
a willingness to confess a wrong spirit
sincerity
a generous spirit
a sympathetic spirit
trusting others
having faith in Christ, not others, but
    expressed as trust to others, knowing that
    we belong to him
joyfulness
prayer
discretion
critical spirit toward oneself
gentle and quiet spirit
humility
using our gifts for one another
remembering our own mistakes
Christ-centeredness
love, in word and deed
fair dealing
integrity
recognizing one's place
a forgiving spirit
doing things decently and in order
conscientiousness
faithfulness
being responsible to perform the tasks
    assigned to us
not misusing our authority over others

That gives us something to work toward, doesn't it? If we are interested in God's will, we will work toward obtaining these positive traits and omitting the negative ones, because the Bible teaches that we are accountable for our conduct.

DISCUSSION QUESTIONS

1. What is the primary difference between the responsibilities of those living under the Old Testament Law and those living now as Christians?

2. How should we react when new believers don't "measure up" to our Christian standards? What are some examples from your own experience?

3. How should we test our convictions?

4. Are there temporary or local expedients you are keeping now in order to maintain unity and peace with other Christians? What are they? Are you able to do (or not do) these things even though you are not really convicted about the matters, and still be at peace within yourself?

5. Look over the lists on pages 112-114. Choose several items from each list that you need to work on. Then begin today to improve your conduct in those areas.

SUGGESTED READING

The World, the Flesh, and the Devil, Harold Lindsell. Canon Press, 1973.
The Measure of a Man, Gene Getz. Regal, n.d.
You Mean the Bible Teaches That, Charles Ryrie. Moody Press, 1974.
Transformed Temperaments, Tim LaHaye. Tyndale, 1971.

God's Will and
Your TV

Television watching must be regulated in your home. It can (due to human weakness) consume much more of your time than is valuable or helpful.

One study concluded, "From ages three through sixteen he (the average child) spends more total time on television than on school. In these years he devotes about one-sixth of all his waking hours to television. In fact, he is likely to devote more time to television than to any other activity except sleep and perhaps play, depending on how play is defined."[1]

Paul Witty, professor emeritus of the School of Education at Northwestern University, has done extensive research into the amount of time youngsters sprawl on the floor before a television set. He tells us, "Children in grades 1-2 spend fifteen to sixteen hours per week watching TV. Total average for elementary school children is twenty-one hours per week. Grades 5-6 spend the most

[1]Wilbur Schramm, Jack Lyle, and Edwin B. Parker, *Television in the Lives of our Children* (Stanford, Calif.: Stanford Press, 1961), p. 30.

time on TV—twenty-five hours per week. High schoolers spend only twelve to fourteen hours per week."

But an A. C. Nielson Company survey showed that in January and February of 1968, the time jumped to an all-time high of forty-six and a half hours per week in the average U.S. home. The most habitual viewers are women over fifty years of age who log an average thirty-three and a half hours before the box each week.

A new survey, *Television and the Public,* written by Robert T. Bower, concludes that we are watching television more but enjoying it less. Based on a national sample of 1,900 people, from age eighteen up, he figures the average viewer spends twenty-eight evening and week-end hours before the set each week, compared with 23.4 hours weekly a decade earlier. Thirty-eight percent of the people think television is getting better, but forty-one percent of the people think it is getting worse. Eighty percent say that TV is more relaxing than not, and two-thirds of the people think it is more "simple-minded" than not. Although the more education a person has, the lower his view of television, the well-educated people watch just as much and watch the same things as the less-educated. As a group, blacks are the most enthusiastic watchers.

Asked whether TV offers enough, not enough, or too much of various types of programming, respondents said there was enough escape (fifty-six percent) and laughs (sixty-one percent), but not enough education (seventy-five percent) or advice (fifty-eight percent). Perhaps the most surprising statistic was the one indicating that seventy-six percent think children are better off with television than without it. Please remember that these figures are *averages.* So some people are watching a lot more to bring the average up so high.

The Director of the Center of Communications at Fordham University points out, "By the time the average American student graduates from high school today, he has watched more than 15,000 hours of television. During the same period, this average student has attended school five hours a day, 180 days a year, for twelve years, to produce a total of 10,800 hours of school time."[2]

"But that's not me," you may be thinking. Now let's be honest. How much time did you spend in front of the TV last week? Begin to figure that movie at two hours, that favorite program each night at thirty minutes or an hour. The football games. The daytime soap operas. Now how much was your television turned on last week for the whole family? Begin to figure your viewing time, your mate's viewing time, the children's cartoons each morning and most of Saturday. You may be surprised at how much you really do watch TV.

And why is it that people don't spend more time in Bible study, family devotions, prayer, and church work? "We don't have enough time." Time is the big problem of our day. We need more time to study the Word and go visiting in the neighborhood for the Lord. But where are we spending our time?

This week try an experiment. Place a pen and paper on top of each TV set in your home. Each time you turn on the set, write down the time. When you turn off the set, mark the time. Keep a log for one week.

Television is one of the most effective communicators in the history of communication. The box doesn't just talk and show, it communicates. What's so bad about that? Simply this: That box is teaching your children, and some of its programs teach things you wouldn't agree with.

Ralph Garry, professor of educational psychology at Boston University, says that television not only affects a child's knowledge but also his concepts and attitudes.[3] One of the biggest problems is the high credibility of TV. Seeing is believing. Children may doubt a parent, min-

[2]John M. Culkin, "Great Movies Go to School," *Saturday Review,* July 16, 1966.

[3]Sylvia Sunderlin (editor), *Children and T.V.,* Chapter 2 (by Ralph Garry), "Television's Impact on the Child," (Washington D.C.: Association for Childhood Education International, 1967), p. 7.

ister, or teacher. But they don't doubt that television. If the TV says this hair spray is best, it's the best.

Television is a great teacher. Unfortunately, "Children do not put education in one category and entertainment in another. A child learns from everything he sees. He learns not so much from what people tell him as from what he sees them actually doing."[4]

One of the most dangerous problems of television's effectiveness is its advertising. Commercials are becoming more numerous on many programs. A Saturday morning program, for instance, will include eighteen to nineteen commercial spots during a one-hour program.

Some years ago a booklet was written to help broadcasters sell air-time to advertisers. The title of the booklet was, "And a Little Child Shall Lead Them—to your product." The pamphlet stated that seventy percent of the kids ask their parents to buy products advertised on television, and that eighty-nine percent of those parents do it. The scheme involves a local hero who "talks to his followers in the vernacular of his own community" and then "shows them a rip-roaring Western movie, introduces neighborhood children to the TV audience, tells a story or two, and sells products!"

The Institute for Propaganda Analysis has listed several gimmicks used by TV advertisers:

1. Bad names, words with unpleasant connotations (bad breath).
2. Glad names, words connected with pleasant feelings (springtime).
3. Transfer, i.e., when you buy a product, you transfer your feelings to it.
4. Testimonial. Well-known persons endorse products (football hero uses certain shaving cream).
5. Plain folks, common man (Colonel Sanders).

---

[4]*Ibid.*, Chapter 8 (by Betty Longstreet and Frank Orme), "The Unguarded Hours," p. 46.

6. Stacking the cards, telling only a part of the truth (product does unclog drains, but it can also eat the pipes).
7. Bandwagon, everybody's doing it.

Another gimmick TV ads use on children and even adults is the inflated price scheme. The TV advertising price is fifty to 100 percent above the actual retail price. The children want the toy but the price is too high. But when the child and the parents see the toy in the store and notice the much lower price, they grab the bargain quickly.

TV must be regulated in your home. The set can gobble up valuable time, time you could spend much more profitably as a believer. If television was not so effective, it would not be nearly so dangerous. But it is effective. It does shape the patterns and habits of your children. The advertisers know that. It's time for parents to learn the facts.

But we must be fair in our evaluation of the one-eyed monster. Much TV programming is clean entertainment or education. Researchers tell us that those who neglect homework to watch TV would neglect homework anyway. One researcher put it this way, "On the basis of the data at hand, we cannot say that heavy television viewing, at any stage of the elementary school, significantly lowers school grades."[5]

Some fear that children read less when they watch more, but some researchers tell us that librarians report an increase in the amount of reading among both elementary and secondary students.

But when the coin is turned over, the statistics show us that for every one hour of reading, there are three given to watching television. The ratio is decidedly lopsided. Alistair Cooke, noted correspondent for "The Guardian"

[5]Joyce Marion Ridder, "Public Opinion and the Relationship of Television Viewing to Academic Achievement," *Journal of Educational Research*, Vol. 5, December 1963.

in England and host of various television series, makes these comments about the impact of television: "The most striking effect is that TV has produced a generation of children who have a declining grasp of the English language, but also have a visual sophistication that was denied to their parents. They learn so much about the world that appeals immediately to their emotions, but I'm not sure it involves their intelligence, their judgment." As far as affecting a child's development today is concerned, he ranks television after parents but "far ahead of school and church."

The purpose of this chapter is not to arouse your anger and suspicions to the point of burning your set. The purpose is balance—regulate what comes into your home.

Who among us did not enjoy, benefit, and learn from watching the first two men on the moon? Let him cast the first stone at the picture tube.

A further reason to regulate the viewing on the goofy-box is that it is dangerous. The airwaves are crammed with violence that spills into your living room or den, and into your children's minds.

Joseph Bayly has some interesting facts and figures concerning violence on TV: "One month after the assassination of Robert F. Kennedy, the National Association for Better Broadcasting surveyed programs televised by the seven stations in Los Angeles. Their findings: 452 homicides and 390 murder attempts portrayed individually in 143 hours of crime-and-horror programming between eight A.M. and midnight during a one-week period. Hundreds of other criminal and violent acts were graphically illustrated during this same period: armed robberies, rape attempts, torture, arson, many forms of aggravated assault, extortion, blackmail. Twenty hours of violent war pictures and thirty hours of incredibly violent programs aired specifically for child audiences were also monitored."[6]

---

[6]Joseph Bayly, "How Tall Is Man," *His,* March 1969.

But even here there is a range of destruction to the viewer. For instance, the old-fashioned Western is much less disturbing to children than crime and detective programs.

Ralph Garry, referred to earlier, says, "The closer aggression gets to real life, the more disturbing it is likely to be. Further, the closer to real life, the greater the possible adoption of such behavior."

Many try to deny that violence seen on the screen rubs off onto the viewer. But the facts show that the effect of aggression and violence arouses rather than discharges hostile aggression. In other words, the viewer does not "get it out of his system" by seeing another person act violently. To the contrary, he feels more need to be violent himself.

To avert public wrath on the subject, broadcasters soothe us with the anodyne that the bad guy always loses and the fellow in the white hat wins the day. But again, research shows us the plain truth. "If children see the bad guy punished, they are not likely to initiate his behavior spontaneously. But they do retain information about how to behave aggressively."[7]

No one today seriously claims that prolonged viewing of crime and violence does not harm the child. It is impossible to cram a child with violence and not expect some of that aggression to spill out. When a child sees murder and muggings as common in life, he begins to believe that such must not be so bad after all. Seeing is believing, you know.

How much violence is on television? Eight out of ten programs contain some violence, says Dr. Eli Rubinstein of the State University of New York at Stony Brook. He says networks are not reducing violence, although they say they are. Dr. George Gerbner of the University of Pennsylvania claims violence has decreased in children's

---

[7]Sunderlin (editor) *Children and TV*, Chapter 3 (By Paul Witty), "Some Research on TV," p. 18.

cartoons, but in these shows it is still far above that in program for adults. Dr. Robert Leibert, also of the State University of New York at Stony Brook, accuses the networks of ignoring the 1972 Surgeon General's Report on the relationship between violence on TV and in real life. Violence continues on television, he believes, because it attracts viewers and thus advertisers. Leo S. Singer, president of the Miracle White Company, who has refused to sponsor violent programs, says he has received 35,000 letters in support of his position.

Some parents realize these things and so allow their children to mostly watch cartoons. Cartoons? Have you watched any of those lately? With very few exceptions, the child is again exposed to violence as a way of life. Who is the winner in the cartoons? The smart-aleck, that's who. Often those in authority are made to be bungling idiots as the child or animal outwits them. Can anyone really be surprised at our national decrease in respect for authority?

Another danger of non-regulated TV is the escape from reality it offers the child.

The experts tell us that less than ten percent of commercial television is reality-oriented. Ralph Garry explains the problem: "The greater the parent-child conflict, the greater the use of television, radio, and motion pictures and the less the use of print."[8] He goes on to say that excessive viewing should be regarded as a danger signal.

The child who wishes to escape from reality has a ready-made friend, the television. TV takes him to never-never land, and that's easier to enjoy than this world of conflict with parents and siblings.

Another dangerous problem of TV for the Christian home is the saturation of programming with the "new morality." One recent program showed some teen-age good-guys who help the police. They caught another

[8]*Ibid.*, Chapter 2, "Television's Impact on the Child," p. 12.

teen in the act of thievery. They didn't turn him in though. The results were almost disastrous to the thief, the good teens, and innocent, non-involved people. In the end everything was written to look nice. But the fact that wrong was done by not turning in the thief was never mentioned. This is the new morality. Wrong can sometimes be right; it depends upon the circumstances. Even the Six Million Dollar Man's good friend, Oscar Goldman, recently admitted he sometimes tells lies because "he has to."

Another recent show was centered around the social evil of racial discrimination. Yet that show's heroes are often drunk and committing adultery. Drunkenness and adultery are shown as fun and never punished. But segregation is viewed as evil. This is the new morality. Beware!

What is the solution to these things? Educational TV gets very little response, according to surveys. And frankly, ETV does not have the appeal of commercial programming. The quality is poor and the low budget system seems to improve very slowly.

The answer, of course, is regulation. But do families regulate the viewing habits of the children? Most evidence shouts "no." One study revealed the following:[9]

1. In the majority of families the young child watches almost as much as he wishes and, for the most part, views programs of his own choice.

2. In the majority of families, mothers make little effort to supervise either program selection by the child or the total amount he watches.

3. In most families, the father has little voice in determining the television behavior of his child.

These things ought not to be. We are responsible before God for our children. We now face a situation where our children are being raised by those who exploit them

---

[9]Robert D. Hess and Harriet Goldman, "Parents' Views of the Effect of Television on Their Children," *Child Development*, Vol. 33, June 1962.

for profit. We are allowing our children to be taught by people who are not qualified to teach. And the worst part is that they are effective communicators.

The TV set is a convenient baby-sitter. The late afternoon is a good example. The children come home from school. Mother is tired and must prepare dinner. Father will be home soon. The kids want attention. The reply too often is, "Don't bother me now, go watch TV." And without knowing who or what, we turn our children over to an unqualified baby-sitter. Often he is one who presents negative forces in our child's development.

But TV is a wonderful tool of entertainment. It keeps us alert to the latest news. It teaches us the good as well as the evil. We are pleased that many Christian organizations make good use of prime time. Who could cast a stone at Billy Graham's use of television?

An information specialist at the National Institute of Health, Arthur McIntire, takes us to task when he says, "It is the duty of parents to set limits, not blame television for shortcomings in their children." How right he is.

To allow a television in your home without regulated viewing is like keeping a refrigerator in the den with the door wide open all of the time. You regulate your child's diet of food. His TV intake should be carefully guarded as well.

But these warnings are not for children only. Christian adults must regulate their viewing also. Too much TV wastes valuable time, causes a compromise of convictions, and fills your mind with the ugly, the awful, and the smut of the world.

May I be so bold as to suggest some practical methods of regulating television?

1. Limit the quantity of TV for yourself and your children. A family with eyeballs glued to the screen is not enjoying one another's company. Spend time with your children, but TV-watching doesn't count. Play games and athletics, and talk with your children.

2. Know what your children are watching. Don't de-

pend on hearsay to decide what is a good program. Watch the program and evaluate it for yourself.

3. No TV before homework and chores are done.

4. Explain and evaluate with your child some commercials which do not represent your Christian philosophy of life.

5. No random watching. Never flip on a set to "see what's on." Use that TV schedule. Select which program you want to see. See it and turn the set off.

Our time, talents, mind, and soul belong to God. Soon this life will be over. Now is the appointed time to do God's work and use all we have to glorify him. Whatsoever you do, do it heartily as unto the Lord.

DISCUSSION QUESTIONS

1. How much time do you and your family spend watching TV each week? Keep close records for one week. After you have an accurate account, evaluate carefully if you and your family are spending too much time watching TV.

2. What are the greatest dangers of TV for children? The greatest benefits?

3. What are some new and creative ways Christian groups could use TV?

4. What can Christians do to change TV programming? What are you personally willing to do?

5. How have you implemented the suggestions on pages 126, 127? Do you have additional suggestions?

SUGGESTED READING

Television in the Lives of our Children, Wilbur Schramm, Jack Lyle, and Edwin B. Parker. Stanford University Press, 1961.

Children and TV., Sylvia Sunderlin. Association for Childhood Education International, 1967.

God's Will and
Your Appearance

Some people don't seem to like the fashions and fads of today. It seems that especially the older generation is howling about the skimpy and tight clothes and the far-out fashions of the younger generation. Even though skirts are creeping downward, the complaints continue.

Christian parents are especially concerned and their cry is, "Immodest, immodest." The Bible does say that the Christian is to be modest. But what does that mean?

Modesty is relative. God's Word is not relative, but the application of that Word may be. The Bible just does not say how long a skirt should be or how tight a sweater should be. You see, modesty changes from generation to generation and from society to society. For instance, Eugene Nida says, "One of the chiefs in the Micronesian Island of Yap forbade any woman coming into the town with a blouse. However, he insisted that all women would have to wear grass skirts reaching almost to the ankles. To the Yapese way of thinking, bare legs are a sign of immodesty, while the uncovered breasts are perfectly proper."[1]

One of the problems is that parents who were young in another era are responsible for determining what is modest for their children living in the "now" generation.

Some of our parents blushed at the sight of a woman's leg above the ankle. Some of us turned our heads if we accidentally saw a woman's knee. But today we certainly must understand that the standards of modesty have changed.

So where can we go for help? How can we determine the bounds and rules for decent dress? The Word of God. Even though modesty is relative, I believe the Bible explains how a believer should dress.

The first principle is that the believer should not dress extravagantly.

> Next, he will judge the haughty Jewish women, who mince along, noses in the air, tinkling bracelets on their ankles, with wanton eyes that rove among the crowds to catch the glances of the men. The Lord will send a plague of scabs to ornament their heads! He will expose their nakedness for all to see. No longer shall they tinkle with self-assurance as they walk. For the Lord will strip away their artful beauty and their ornaments, their necklaces and bracelets and veils of shimmering gauze. Gone shall be their scarves and ankle chains, headbands, earrings, and perfumes; their rings and jewels, and party clothes and negligees and capes and ornate combs and purses; their mirrors, lovely lingerie, beautiful dresses and veils. Instead of smelling of sweet perfume, they'll stink; for sashes they'll use

---

[1]Eugene Nida, *Customs and Cultures* (New York: Harper and Row Publishers, Inc., 1954), p. 1.

ropes; their well-set hair will all fall out; they'll wear sacks instead of robes. All their beauty will be gone; all that will be left to them is shame and disgrace. Their husbands shall die in battle; the women, ravaged, shall sit crying on the ground (Isaiah 3:16-26).

This passage is concerned with the extravagant attire of the daughters of Zion or the women in Jerusalem. Remember now, these people are about to be taken into captivity, and they are worried about their attire.

The Word of the Lord condemns these women for putting on too much. (Some mothers of teen-age girls today would like to have that problem.) These Jerusalem women were guilty of overdoing it, being concerned with fancy clothes.

Furthermore, they were rebuked for the expense involved. The attire described here is very expensive. Perfume, rings, and jewelry were not worn by the majority of the ladies.

The point here seems to be that these women were guilty of pride concerning their clothes. They were obviously placing attire too high on the priority list.

Notice that there is not a condemnation of the clothes in this passage. There is nothing sinful in a garment. Matter is not evil.

But the believer should carefully select his clothes. A believer can allow the love of clothes to become a substitute for the love of God. Remember, money is not evil, but the love of money may be. Clothes are not evil, but the love of clothes may be. Clothes and fashions can dominate one's thinking. Even Christians can waste much time and energy wanting something new or fashionable. And, of course, the boys can have the disease as badly as the girls. Some people feel they must keep up with the "in" thing.

A Christian can allow the love of clothes to rob God. Already teen-age girls in this country hand five and a half billion dollars a year across the counter for cosmetics. I have wondered, if each of us would be content with only two pairs of shoes, and assuming we could return all our other pairs and regain the original retail value and donate that to missions, how long would it take to evangelize the world? Many Christians who never consider adding another $20.00 to the check they write for the Sunday offering will spend $30.00 for a new dress which they don't even need.

A Christian can allow the love of clothes to take God's time. Every day and far into the night, the downtown stores and the shopping centers are crowded with people. Some of these people are Christians who undoubtedly spend more time looking at display windows than they do reading their Bible, praying, and attending church.

Love for clothes can be a tool of Satan and can rob you of God's best for your life.

There are some specific principles for buying clothes. First, clothes should be modest. More about that in a moment. Second, clothes should be durable. A Christian should purchase clothes of good quality (and these aren't limited to certain brand names). Some people just like to "drop the names" of the places they buy and the brands they wear. I even knew of one lady who would sew labels from expensive stores into her husband's suits. "It's more impressive for business purposes, you know." Some people seem to really enjoy draping a coat with well-known label across a pew. Clothes should be durable, but be careful that your pride doesn't toss you off balance here.

Also, buy clothes you can afford. Surely there will be Christians who will have to answer to God for the money they spent on clothes. And, as you might expect, most often those who spend the greater amounts on clothes are those who just cannot seem to afford to follow God's biblical pattern of giving.

Clothes for the Christian should also be fashionable. It's not spiritual to look dowdy. One humorist said that you can always tell a Christian because he is five years behind the styles. I believe that every Christian should be as well-dressed and fashionable as the rest of the socio/economic group into which God has placed him.

When women first began ratting their hair and back-combing became popular, many Christian women were aghast. But now those hair styles are quite accepted, and most Christian ladies see nothing wrong in following those styles.

The same is true of colored stockings. There was a time when some Christians thought that colored hosiery made a woman look like a street-walker. But that isn't true now, and colored stockings are worn by many conscientious Christian women.

When the hemlines began to rise a few years ago, some ladies pointed and gulped. Most of those same ladies raised their hemlines for a time before the fashion was to lower them again.

Some may disagree with these principles and quote verses dealing with separation. But those verses dealing with separation have to do with a Christian's attitude and value system.

As Christians we look to our Lord Jesus as our example. How did Jesus dress when he became a man and dwelt among us?

> Upon His head He must always have worn the turban, the national headgear, used alike by rich and poor. The turban He wore was probably white. It was fastened under the chin by a cord, and at the side fell down to the shoulders and over the tunic. Under His turban He wore His hair rather long, and His beard uncut. His tunic, the underneath vesture, was of one piece without seam. It was therefore of some value, and had probably been given Him by one of the women who "ministered to Him of their substance." Over

this He wore the talith, loose and flowing. This mantle was not white, for we are told it became white during transfiguration. It was not red, for that was only the military color; it is possible it was blue, for blue was then very common; or it may have simply been white with brown stripes. In any case, Jesus had at the four corners of this mantle, the ciccith (fringe) . . . He wore sandals on His feet, as we learn from John the Baptist; and when He was traveling, going from place to place, He doubtless wore a girdle around the loins, and carried a stick in His hand.[2]

In other words, Christ dressed like everyone else. His clothes were not out of style, nor did he call attention to himself by means of a false modesty.

The second word I find in Scripture concerning attire is 1 Timothy 2:8-10. The principle here is that the believer should dress modestly. "So I want men everywhere to pray with holy hands lifted up to God, free from sin and anger and resentment. And the women should be the same way, quiet and sensible in manner and clothing. Christian women should be noticed for being kind and good, not for the way they fix their hair or because of their jewels or fancy clothes."

The believer should dress like he prays ("the same way"). One should dress looking to God for guidance. This is seen in the phrase "pray with holy hands." This shows dependence upon God. This matter of dress is important. You need to make this a matter of serious discussion with God.

One should also choose his clothes in the proper spirit. This is seen in the phrase "free from sin and anger." Any Christian who declares he will wear a certain garment just

---

[2]Edmond Stapfer, *Palestine in the Time of Christ* (New York: A. C. Armstrong and Son, 1885).

to show someone his liberty, is not choosing his clothes in the proper spirit. Sometimes teen-agers choose clothes they know their parents won't like. This may even be on a subconscious level, but it is still hostility. The Scriptures say we aren't to choose clothes on that basis.

The passage also teaches that one should choose clothes which honor God. This doesn't mean that dresses must reach the floor or that long sleeves are necessary. I fail to see how this kind of false modesty (and often hypocrisy) honors God at all. Who looks at a person out of style and has his mind turned toward God?

Before going on to verse nine, I think we should define the word modesty. The unabridged Random House Dictionary has this definition: Humble estimate of one's merits or importance; free from vanity, egotism, boastfulness, or showy extravagance; moderate; regard for decencies of behavior, speech, dress.

From this definition it is clear to see that modesty deals with motive. We are concerned not only with what we wear, but also why we wear what we wear. And please remember, you cannot see another's motive.

Modesty is relative. We cannot use verse nine to condemn pigtails, earrings, or a string of pearls. In fact, modesty has nothing to do with the amount of clothing which is worn. Eugene Nida tells us:

> It is taken for granted by most people that those primitive tribes who wear little or no clothing must feel some hidden shame. So far as can be determined, they have no such sense of shame, but on the other hand, regard the wearing of clothes as being exceedingly peculiar. It is true that when such people become Christian converts, they do put on clothing, often in an indescribably ludicrous way; but that does not necessarily mean that they had any inherent shame formerly nor that they regard clothes as a necessary part of Christi-

anity, though they are often told that such is the case. For them the wearing of certain types of clothing is just a matter of conformance to other standards. Clothing provides social acceptance and a feeling of identification with the prestige-laden foreign culture, but it may or may not be a response to spiritual convictions. On the basis of very wide observation and study, it can be said that there is no correlation between the amount of clothing which people wear and their standards of morality. However, in any one society those who are "modest"—in terms of the local system of etiquette—are more likely to be moral than those who do not so conform. Nevertheless, a person may be modest in terms of the amount or kind of clothing and yet be a sexual exhibitionist.[3]

One of the arguments against skimpy clothing is that exposure of a girl's leg two or three inches above the knee stirs the emotions and passions of the boys. But I am not at all convinced that the sight of a girl's leg two or three inches above the knee does any more to a young man now than the sight of the knee did a generation ago.

I find two principles in verse nine. Clothes for the believer should be neat and becomimg. This kind of attire suits a Christian best. This is the opposite of luxurious and costly. What worldly women attempt to gain through costly clothes and ornamentation, the Christian woman seeks through good works.

The Bible explains how a believer should dress. One of the reasons we should carefully select our clothes is because there is a certain amount of truth to the axiom, "An individual's dress is a mirror of his mind." The word from this passage for the believer is "modesty" (KJV).

---

[3]Nida, *Customs*, pp. 89, 90.

LIVE
CONFIDENTLY
[136]

The emphasis of modesty is upon action more than attire. The word "sobriety" (KJV) indicates self-control. The word has the connotations of dignity and seriousness of purpose.

The Greek word used here for modesty (KJV) stresses good behavior. This is the same word which is translated in 1 Timothy 3:2, "good behavior." The word in secular Greek included the idea of control of the body and its movements.

We all know that the same dress on two different women with the same build and weight may look entirely different because of the bodily movements of the women in the dress. A woman doesn't have to walk like a field hand at the end of a day of picking cotton, but it just isn't necessary to move as much sideways as forward when one walks.

In the past decade, there has been a lot of flak about the length of a man's hair. All this bickering about how Jesus looked (both sides claim he wore his hair like they prefer) really doesn't answer the questions. The references to great preachers of the past who wore long hair, and the identification of long hair with the hippie movement and rebellion don't help either.

Again, we need to see principles from the Bible. It is true that 1 Corinthians 11:14 says that it is a shame for a man to have long hair. But how long is long? There is one simple principle: Men shouldn't look like women, and women shouldn't look like men.

So when is a boy's hair too long? When he could be mistaken for a girl. When is it wrong for a girl to wear jeans? When she could be mistaken for a boy. The issue deals with the individual in his own culture at the time the decision is made.

Have you ever wondered why the Bible just doesn't come out and say yea or nay? Why didn't God just say, "No shorter than two inches above the knee"? The reason is that God is bringing each of us through a process of maturity. We would never be able to mature and grow and learn and make our own decisions to honor God if we only kept a list of rules and regulations.

So God has placed principles in the Bible through which we can discern his will for our appearance. Sometimes we have to study and dig out the truth piece by piece, but that's how we learn and that's how we grow, and that's how we discover his will.

DISCUSSION QUESTIONS

1. What is modest dress for Christian ladies in your circle of friends or church? For men?

2. Practically speaking, how should a Christian discover the balance between being extreme, extravagant, and dowdy in appearance?

3. Evaluate the amount of time and money you spend on clothes. Do you waste time shopping? Do you buy unnecessarily? What steps can you take to improve the problem? If another Christian has this problem, how can you help?

4. What does one's attitude have to do with one's appearance?

5. How do you evaluate the hair length issue? Does the one principle on page 137 seem reasonable? Why? Why not? Evaluate the "unisex look" in light of this principle.

SUGGESTED READING

Strictly Feminine, Marti Hefley. Victor Books, 1973.
The Total Woman, Marabel Morgan. Fleming Revell, 1973.